A Dose of Devotion

How Couples Living With Multiple Sclerosis Keep Their Love Strong

By Ronda Giangreco

& Jeanne Lassard

ISBN-13: 978-1503055049
ISBN-10: 1503055043

True love is not a strong, fiery, impetuous passion. It is, on the contrary, an element calm and deep. It looks beyond mere externals, and is attracted by qualities alone. It is wise and discriminating, and its devotion is real and abiding.

Ellen G. White

Table of Contents

Prologue

∂

"You have Multiple Sclerosis."

It is a terrifying moment when you first hear those words. Understandably, how the disease will damage your body is your immediate concern. But seldom do we take into consideration how destructive a chronic illness often is to a marriage.

It can be tremendously difficult for a couple to accept that the active, adventure-filled future they imagined they would enjoy has been altered or perhaps lost forever. The love that brought them together often crumbles under the weight of such a loss.

And yet some couples manage to develop an even more intense love for one another when faced with such disheartening news. Their commitment deepens and grows more meaningful than they ever imagined possible. Multiple Sclerosis doesn't end their love story. Remarkably, their marriage matures into an even richer and more emotionally rewarding relationship.

Much has been written about the factors that cause marriages to fail when Multiple Sclerosis enters the picture. There has been very little written about the reasons some of them succeed. Success in marriage, especially those beset with health challenges is an art.

We decided to go directly to some of the best artists we could find to share with you the secrets to their marital masterpieces. In this collection of interviews with couples who battle this illness every day you will read the ways in which they manage to keep their love strong. They share their most intimate struggles and most triumphant victories. The couples and individuals who were interviewed have realized that there is no way to get around the diagnosis and subsequent trials. They have accepted the fact that they must simply endure them, and they do so arm-in-arm, as partners and as lovers. When one of them feels as though the burden is too much, the other gladly accepts more of the load. Their expertise at creating and maintaining a balance between giving and taking is a skill they have mastered, along with the ability to communicate their feelings and needs.

It is our sincere hope that through their stories others will find their own path toward a relationship that is filled with many doses of devotion.

Why Devotion Is Vital To Your Health & Happiness

"Shared sorrow is half sorrow, shared joy is double joy."
Swedish Proverb

Marriage can be difficult under the best of conditions. Needless to say, Multiple Sclerosis is hardly the best of conditions.

The daily challenges that become part of a marriage when Multiple Sclerosis enters the picture require both partners to make considerable adjustments. Roles can become blurred and confused. Loyalty and patience is tested on a daily, even hourly basis. Sometimes even the basic truths that you thought you knew about one another can fall into doubt.

It is during times of trouble that you discover your partner's true nature. Chronic, progressive illness creates more than a relationship's fair share of those times. But what you learn may not always be what you expected.

Nearly everyone has heard the disappointing statistic that fifty percent of marriages end in divorce. An even more sobering fact is that when you add a chronic illness such as Multiple Sclerosis into the equation that number can rise to over seventy percent. There are many reasons for this spike in the divorce rate among couples who deal with the sometimes tragic consequences of MS. Some of them are obvious and others may be more unique and personal.

When you are struggling with Multiple Sclerosis it is often the inability to do the things that you were previously able to do that causes the most distress. You may feel embarrassed when you must ask for help. It can seem like an admission of defeat, a white flag waved in the war against MS. It's also easy to become a bit self-absorbed when you are living with a chronic illness. Your needs take precedent. Everyone's attention is focused on you. And while their concern can be reassuring and supportive, at times you can also begin to feel like you are suffocating under the weight of their sympathy.

As a caregiver it's normal to feel resentment toward the illness and all the ways it has changed your life. The sacrifices that it forces you to make can be a constant source of frustration. "This isn't what I signed up for" is a common feeling. Often there is a huge shift of responsibilities onto the shoulders of the caregiver. The pressure to keep everything afloat when your partner isn't feeling well can lead to overwhelming bouts of stress and anxiety. You feel powerless against an adversary as formidable as Multiple Sclerosis.

A recent study by Northwest University followed 121 MS patients for four years. The subjects underwent monthly interviews in which they rated the factors that elevated their stress levels. Amongst all of the stress causing events, relationship troubles were rated the highest, higher even than a death in the family. Those who experienced turmoil in their relationships were also more likely to have enhanced lesions on their MRI scans.

Also, it is well documented that depression is a major issue for those diagnosed with Multiple Sclerosis. Studies have found that a healthy marriage reduces depressive symptoms for both men and women. It was discovered that getting married decreases depressive symptoms in most patients, while getting divorced increases them. Sadly, the prevalence of depressive symptoms due to divorce remains elevated for *years* after the marriage breaks up.

In short, a marriage lacking in devotion can be absolutely devastating for a person with Multiple Sclerosis.

But is it possible that a loving marriage can contribute both to the well-being of the ill spouse as well as their partner? The answer seems to be a resounding *yes!*

According to an article published in the Journal of the Royal Society of Medicine, "Many studies have identified positive aspects of the role, with partners describing increased self-esteem, pride, gratification and feeling closer to their spouse." One researcher even suggested that, "The responsibility of caring for one's ill partner may confer a sense of meaning to life and this in turn may augment global quality of life."

In another study of the spouses of Multiple Sclerosis patients, researchers found that many of the partners reported that being a caregiver had actually made them more caring towards others in general.

We know that a good marriage can have a positive effect on both partners. Multiple Sclerosis does not change that fact. The union can still provide many advantages and benefits. Love itself is powerful medicine, releasing endorphins that are natural pain killers, as well as anti-depressants. Oxytocin is also produced in large quantities when we are hugged or caressed. And finally, phenyl ethylamine, another hormone that becomes elevated when we are in a loving marriage has been proven to increase blood flow and to elicit feelings of euphoria.

Even more amazing is that when researchers subjected married women to the threat of an electric shock they discovered that when the women were holding their husband's hand they showed less response in the brain areas associated with stress.

Simply put, humans are wired to feel connected to one another. We are at our best when we are loved. Illness doesn't change that. In fact, it can amplify both the need and the benefits of a close and caring relationship.

But the rewards of attaining a marriage full of devotion aren't simply limited to what each spouse experiences. Society as a whole reaps a payback.

Studies show that the likelihood of a woman having a best-case outcome with her disease depends, in part, on the health of her marriage. One recent report found that women in distressed relationships recovered more slowly, and they also experienced more symptoms of illness and more side effects from treatment.

Researchers have also found that married people have fewer doctor's visits and shorter average hospital stays. As well, with a happy marriage you are amongst the demographic with the healthiest blood pressure, a vital factor in overall health.

During a recent experiment, researchers at Ohio State University Medical Center purposely gave married couples small blister wounds. The wounds healed nearly twice as fast for spouses who interacted with warmth and concern, compared with those who demonstrated hostility toward one another.

According to Harry Reis, PhD, co-editor of the Encyclopedia of Human Relationships, married people live longer because they feel connected and loved. "Nobody quite knows why loving relationships are good for health. The best logic for this is that human beings have been crafted by evolution to live in closely knit social groups. When that is not happening, the biological systems get overwhelmed."

Chip & Jeanne Allen

W hether or not you believe in love at first sight there is no denying the mysterious laws of attraction. For Jeanne Allen, it was a distinguished older man wearing a pink shirt that caused her heart to flutter. She and a girlfriend had just boarded an airplane bound for Club Med in Mexico. After arriving at the resort, she found herself scanning the crowd for the man who had been seated a few rows in front of her, hoping to catch his eye. Little did she know that she already had? How could he miss her? A tall, willowy woman with striking blue eyes, Jeanne stood out even in a crowd of beautiful, young vacationers roaming the resort grounds.

The first words exchanged between them, however, were hardly romantic. Jeanne and her girlfriend had arrived late to a variety show. When she heard someone beside her roughly say, "Could you get out of my way?" she turned around and found herself face to face with that handsome guy from the airplane. Even though it was not quite the introduction she was hoping for, she thought to herself, "Contact has been made!"

Jeanne: I asked him, "Weren't you on the plane with us from Los Angeles?" He told me that he was actually on the plane with me all the way from San Francisco. That's when I knew that he had noticed me as well. He even remembered what I had been wearing.

Chip: Funny thing is, as we would later learn, neither of us are normally very observant people.

That evening they ended up dancing the night away together and soon became somewhat of an "item" at Club Med. However, there was a nagging concern in the back of Jeanne's mind.

Jeanne: He was from San Francisco, and after several evenings together, he still hadn't kissed me. And then there was that pink shirt.

Chip: I can't believe she thought I was gay! I'm just shy!

Upon returning home, Jeanne gave Chip her phone number and waited patiently for him to call. She told her co-workers that she really believed that she may have found "the one". But after three days went by with no phone call, she began to worry that perhaps it simply had been a vacation romance, nothing more than the sparks that fly when there's sun, sand and tequila involved. What she had no way of knowing was that Chip needed some extra time before phoning her. He was diligently trying to plan the perfect romantic evening.

Chip: This was one date that I really wanted to make special.

A friend at his company happened to have tickets to the symphony that she wasn't able to use, and he decided that an evening of beautiful music would set just the right mood for their first stateside night together.

Jeanne: Finally on Wednesday I got the call and the invitation to the Symphony in San Francisco. Needless to say, I spent quite a bit of time on my wardrobe selection for the evening, wanting to find the perfect look for this elegant date. Little did I know that we would begin the evening by enjoying ribs at "Hog Heaven".

Chip: She was a great sport about my choice in a restaurant but her faith in my ability to plan the perfect date was about to be severely tested.

Unbeknownst to Chip, or his coworker, the tickets that he purchased from her had actually been stolen. When the rightful seat holders showed up and demanded that Chip and Jeanne move the couple was fortunately able to coax a sympathetic usher into allowing them to sit in some unsold seats. Their budding relationship was saved. Many less traumatic dates would follow.

On July 3rd of 1986, on a dinner cruise in the San Francisco Bay, Chip asked Jeanne to marry him. It would become their tradition for the next twenty-seven years to toast the evening with a different water view every year.

Jeanne: We made the vow that we would always celebrate that moment while gazing upon a serene vista involving a body of water. It proved to be a task that sometimes required elaborate planning.

Chip: One year we were in Missouri visiting her mother and in order to find water we had to make a detour to the Grand Lake of the Cherokees in Oklahoma. Have you ever tried to create a romantic evening at a Smorgasbord, complete with an old guy playing cheesy music on a keyboard for ambiance?

Jeanne: Of course, that's the year we remember the most!

In May of 1987, they said their vows. Unfortunately, the joy and excitement of beginning their new life together

18

corresponded with some unsettling news. Jeanne had experienced several incidents in the previous year of inexplicable numbness in her right leg. But each time the troubling symptom appeared, before she could get any answers, it disappeared again.

> *Once you've got a name for your symptoms then you can do something about it. If you don't know who your enemy is, how can you fight it?*

Chip: I honestly thought that there was a simple explanation for this. Jeanne was traveling a lot and she was lugging suitcases through the airport. I was sure it was just a simple case of sciatica.

The answer would prove to be much more troubling.

Jeanne: When the neurologist that we went to see threw out the words "Multiple Sclerosis", it made me angry. Why would they suggest something that serious?

Additional testing would prove that Multiple Sclerosis had indeed come into their life. The answer also came with a lot of questions for each of them. But one thing that was never in question was how they would handle this obstacle. They would face it together.

Chip: When we learned the truth the first thought that came to me was that this was just something we'd deal with. I knew that it could involve a rapid degeneration. I could deal with that. But what I couldn't deal with was the thought of losing her. Anything but that. My agreement with myself was that this is the woman I love and I was going to do whatever I need to do.

Jeanne: I think I was relieved when I finally knew what I had. Once you've got a name for your symptoms, then you can do something about it. If you don't know who your enemy is, how can you fight it?

For the next several years Jeanne was in what she called "healthy denial." After going to a couple of support group meetings, she decided that they weren't for her.

Jeanne: I looked around the room at people in walkers and wheelchairs. I wasn't even using a cane back then. I said to myself, "that's them, it's not me." I was going to just keep on living my life because why wouldn't I? I didn't belong there. And I thought I never would.

But Jeanne's ability to remain in healthy denial began to wane as the evidence of MS's impact became too much to ignore. The couple had long enjoyed the hobby of biking. It was becoming painfully obvious that this was a part of their life they may soon have to give up.

Chip: Jeanne would ride until she simply couldn't pedal any further. That is so Jeanne. She just wasn't going to stop. But eventually we realized she could not ride by herself anymore. That's when a friend suggested a tandem bike. We went down to our local bike shop to give it a try. While out on a ride, a woman passed us and made the comment, "If my husband and I were riding that we would be divorced!"

Jeanne: That tandem bike was actually a miracle worker. I would recommend that every couple have one, disabled or not. With a tandem bike, it is essential that you work in unison, communicate effectively and most of all, be supportive of one another. What a recipe for a successful relationship!

Chip: The bike allowed us to continue to do something we loved in spite of Jeanne's limitations. I was so proud of Jeanne. She got to the point where it was a source of pride that when she got off the bike and whipped out her cane, people would stop and stare in admiration.

Jeanne: I was determined that I was going to live a normal life. And I am still living a normal life, just a slightly different version of normal.

The relationship skills they honed while riding a tandem bike would prove to be very useful in dealing with the hurdles that were ahead of them.

While Jeanne's decline was gradual, by the time she reached her fifties it was clear that her mobility issues were becoming more severe. She went from using a cane, to a walker, and finally to a wheelchair.

Chip: I am in awe of Jeanne all of the time. She is the ultimate fighter. She is never going to quit. It may have been healthy denial in the beginning, but we always find a way to deal with the curveballs that this disease throws us.

Jeanne: In the early years I thought Chip would be embarrassed by my disability. Here I was, a forty something year old woman walking with a cane or a walker. He was in the prime of his life and I am looking like a ninety year old. I kept waiting for him to act uncomfortable with it all, but he never did.

Even with the assistance the mobility tools provided her, just getting from one place to another was never going to be enough for such an active woman as Jeanne. The adventurous nature she and Chip shared would ultimately put them on a path to both new places and an exciting business venture. The desire to travel, in spite of the challenges of Multiple Sclerosis, would become the inspiration for a website aimed at helping people with disabilities to travel with confidence.

Jeanne: As a disabled woman, when I plan trips I research my destination for hours on the internet and the phone. "Accessible" is a start but it doesn't help me find the handicap entrance or tell me how often the bus with the lift runs. It's frustrating.

Their accessible travel planning website is designed for people with limited mobility, from those who have difficulty walking to people in wheelchairs. The site allows the disabled community to travel with confidence and provides them with travel tips and itinerary suggestions in the California wine country.

With the creation of their new business, the loss of her former career as a fashion buyer was no longer a painful memory. Working long hours and climbing the corporate ladder, as well as the stress of her job had been a factor in accelerating her disease progression. But this new endeavor was fun!

The accessible travel business gave her a way to help others and to use the information she and Chip had gathered through their many explorations.

Jeanne: I've gained all of this knowledge about accessible travel and for years I'd done nothing with it. It was time to share it and create a website. I wanted to tell others about a great restaurant that didn't have a handicap entrance through the kitchen. I want to feature a wonderful hotel and let people know that the shower is reachable from the shower bench. I want tell others about a scenic boat tour in which "accessible" meant a ramp, not a couple of guys hauling me onboard!

Chip: While I certainly wish that Jeanne had never gotten MS, without the presence of this disease in our life I would have never realized how strong she really is. I have to take naps, she just keeps going. I sometimes wonder if our life would have been different, but I'm not sure it would be. We find ways to do the things we love. We may not do them as quickly as everyone else, but we still get to experience wonderful things together.

Jeanne: Chip had always loved the town of Sonoma. Now that I no longer needed to commute into the city from Oakland and Chip could practice law from anywhere, it seemed like a perfect time to make the move. I guess you could say that Multiple Sclerosis brought us to paradise.

The paradise of the wine country was just the place to launch their website too. The couple created the first handicap accessible travel guide to Northern California's Wine Country. In her online videos Jeanne explores the area on her scooter, visiting accessible wineries, historical sites, hotels and restaurants.

Chip: We were working crazy hours and we never saw one another. Now I work out of our home and Jeanne is often here all day. We enjoy the simple pleasure of spending time together. We eat breakfast, lunch and dinner at the same table. We share special moments throughout the day. If she had gone on with her career, and I was doing my law practice at a big firm, we would see so much less of each other on a daily basis. It is odd to think that something as awful as Multiple Sclerosis has actually helped us to be such devoted companions. We've learned that we enjoy life so much more when we're together.

Even with her intrepid spirit, having Chip close at hand has been a godsend for Jeanne as her disease made it necessary for her to lean on him even more than she ever had before.

Jeanne: It took me awhile to learn that I needed to ask for help. I remember that I would be doing something and it would be so hard. I would be thinking, "Why can't you see how difficult this is for me? Why aren't you helping me?" Maybe because we know each other so well I just expected him to realize when I was struggling. I finally came to the conclusion that he wasn't a mind reader and I should tell him what I needed.

Chip: I was trying to make sure that I wasn't over-protecting. I have learned to let Jeanne do as much as she can on her own, but I probably cross the line every now and then.

In spite of the devotion they shared, inevitably they would sometimes mourn the loss of the things they could no longer do together.

Jeanne: Of all the things the things I miss most about the days before MS entered our lives, it is walking hand-in-hand down the beach. We don't get to do that anymore. I see couples holding each other's hand and not even thinking about it. We can't hold hands like that anymore and never will again. Change the picture - boy and girl walking hand-in hand to girl sitting in wheelchair and boy pushing her.

Chip: I have tried holding her hand when she's in the scooter and it's just not the same. Though we can't walk on the beach together, we still stop and spend those moments looking at the ocean or the sun setting. It's still one of the things that we enjoy more than anything else in the world.

While idyllic hand-in-hand strolls on the beach may have become a thing of the past, the two have developed their own method for enjoying another favorite romantic activity.

Jeanne: Believe it or not, we can still dance! It has taken us a while to figure out how to do it, but we have now perfected the art of "stand dancing". Chip holds me up and keeps me from falling over while we sort of just sway to the music. Those are some very intimate and tender moments for us.

Chip: There's one song we both really love, a song about friends and lovers. It expresses what our relationship is all about.

Multiple Sclerosis may have changed many things about Chip and Jeanne's life, but it didn't change a single thing about who they are and how much they love one another.

Jeanne: Yes, things would have been different if I had not contracted this disease. My career would have probably flourished and we would have a lot more money now. But we'd have less of other assets that are, in the long run, much more important. I think MS magnifies who you are, your inherent qualities, and even more importantly, your core relationship. Chip and I have always believed that if you follow your passion, success will come to you. And then we look at each other and say the only thing I am truly passionate about is you!

Jenifer & Don Walsh

To a great extent the bond between Jenifer and Don Walsh has been forged by Multiple Sclerosis. Many would consider that to be a sad statement. But Don and Jenifer would never think of their marriage as one plagued by misfortune. While MS may have caused them to struggle with many challenges, it has also given the couple a mission in life, a passion for fundraising, and a love story that has inspired an entire community.

While Multiple Sclerosis was destined to play a major role in their life as a couple, unbeknownst to them it was waiting in the wings before they even met. Jenifer just didn't have a name for the strange bouts of numbness that seemed to appear and then vanish without explanation.

Jenifer: I was working for an insurance company and living with my sister. One morning I noticed that the big toe on my right foot had fallen asleep. Oddly, the feeling didn't go away for days. Then suddenly it was gone. It was a strange episode, but honestly, I didn't think much of it. But then it started happening to my whole foot. My sister is a physical therapist and she kept insisting that I call a doctor, but always before I could make an appointment the sensation disappeared. Besides, I didn't even know what kind of doctor to call. One morning though I woke up and went to take a shower. Suddenly, I felt like I was cut in half. The whole right side of my body was numb. My sister and I were freaking out and she told me to go see a neurologist. I made an appointment that day.

Unfortunately an answer as to what was causing her strange symptoms would be a long time coming. It took an entire decade between when she first realized something was seriously wrong and the day that her doctor finally delivered the news that she had Multiple Sclerosis. During that time, her physicians would rule out Lyme disease, lupus, transverse myelitis, and meningitis. But they pointedly never ruled out MS.

Jenifer: They never really talked about Multiple Sclerosis in detail, but unlike the other possibilities, they never said I didn't have it either. Toward the end of ten years of testing they started talking about it more seriously.

During these years Jenifer wasn't totally focused on her health though. After all, she was a young woman in her twenties and anxious to meet the man of her dreams. When a friend offered to set her up on a blind date with a wonderful guy she worked out with at a local gym, Jenifer readily agreed.

The dinner date went well. He had thoughtfully brought her flowers and over the course of the evening they discovered that they shared much in common.

Don: We learned that we had very similar values. We both come from close-knit, Roman Catholic families. That was important to us. We agreed that if you don't have similar values it will never work. Our religion plays a big role in our life. Two of my three sisters are nuns.

Jenifer: After a few dates I told my sister, "Oh my god, this guy is so nice." He is a gemologist and even though I am not a jewelry person, when he created this little bumble bee especially for me I was so blown away.

In spite of the growing affection between them there were the concerns about her health lingering in the background of their budding romance.

Don: It's not something you bring up on a first date, but as we started getting more serious she began telling me about what was happening to her. She even told me about one episode when she was bedridden for a week. Naturally, I was worried about her. We talked about it often. One of the things she said to me was that there was a chance she could be diagnosed with MS. She could end up in a wheelchair. I didn't care because by that time I knew that I loved her. I even went to a lot of her appointments with her. The worst one was the spinal tap. It was horrible to see her going through that. And then she developed a spinal headache. You never want to see someone you love suffer like that.

With the exception of Jenifer's on-again, off-again symptoms and numerous doctor's appointments, the two went on with their active lives. Both Jenifer and Don are extremely sports-minded, physical people. They weren't about to let a few bouts of numbness and some troubling talk of illness slow them down.

Jenifer: Don was a runner and he had even run two marathons before we met. As a new girlfriend, you want to join your boyfriend in his pursuits so I took up running. We were training for a half marathon and my knee kept bothering me. I even started wearing a brace. I didn't know what was wrong, it was just bothering me. I really wanted to do that half marathon so I pushed through the discomfort. When I look back, I think I knew that MS had something to do with my problems.

Pushing aside their concerns about the future the two became engaged and then enjoyed a typical big, boisterous Catholic wedding with their large, extended family. It was a joyful time in their life. Soon they learned they were expecting a baby. But their delight over the pregnancy would be over-shadowed by some terrible news. A new round of testing confirmed the doctor's previous suspicions. There was no longer any doubt. Jenifer had Multiple Sclerosis.

Jenifer: Here I was pregnant and my doctor was giving me drugs because I had an episode. I was so freaked out that something was going to happen to my baby. They kept assuring me that it would be fine, though.

Don: It was one of the most exciting times of our lives, but it was a very difficult time as well. We were only married two years and our emotions were all over the place. At least now we knew what was wrong. Jenifer had been going through years of testing for this and testing for that. Now we were having a child and we had to figure out a way to fight this. My greatest fear was how was I going to be able to take care of a wife and a young child if she became totally handicapped? I had worked with a woman who had Primary Progressive MS. She had passed away from the disease. I wanted to get some assurance from the neurologist that this was not the same type because I needed to start making plans. I need to take care of things. I'm the type of person who will assess a situation and then figure out how to handle it. I grew up in a very close family. We had a number of problems and I saw how my parents dealt with

31

them. I learned that you cope with what is before you and you move on with your life. I explained to Jenifer that this is how we would handle Multiple Sclerosis. We wouldn't let it rule our lives.

But for Jenifer, her growing concerns that she might not be able to care for her child were consuming her. At a time when she should have been able to thoroughly enjoy the pregnancy she had so wanted, she was grief-stricken at the thought that she might not be around to watch her child grow.

Jenifer: My biggest fear was that I had a baby inside me and I was so afraid of what was happening to both of us. Would I be able to care for this baby? When I read about what MS was and what could happen to you, I was devastated. But that's when I also discovered that I am a very strong person.

Their daughter, Cara was born was premature but healthy.

Jenifer: I thought maybe her premature birth had something to do with my disease, but the doctors assured me that it didn't. She was in the hospital for close to two weeks. I was all set up to go back to work and had daycare arrangements made, but she needed me. With the attention a tiny baby required and my increasingly troublesome health concerns, I never ended up going back to work. That was difficult for us financially.

A few years later the couple also welcomed a son into their family. As they grew, the couple's children became aware of their mother's challenges.

Don: We chose not to hide this from anybody, including our children. Some people keep it from their kids and don't want them to know. We felt just the opposite. Jenifer would have at least one attack a year that would knock her down for a couple weeks. We couldn't really hide that. We felt it was important to let people know what was going on. Jenifer was determined to lead her life as normally as she possibly could.

Jennifer: Multiple Sclerosis, sadly, has been a part of my children's life from the moment they were born. But honestly, I think it has provided them with some wonderful life lessons. Others tell us all the time how compassionate our children are. Acts of thoughtfulness, like holding the door for a person with a cane, just seems to come naturally to them. They are totally in tune with and aware of the needs of others. We are so proud when we hear from their teachers that they are such caring young people.

For many years it would have been easy to miss the fact that Jenifer was struggling with MS, but as Jenifer's mobility has declined she has required more assistance from her loving family.

Don: All of her friends think that she's extremely strong. She doesn't really let her guard down with them. But she does let it down with me. I want her to because you can't be strong and upbeat and positive all the time. I know how vulnerable she feels sometimes.

Jenifer: My ability to walk is progressively getting worse. I am very affected on my right side. If I don't pay attention I walk toe first and fall. I try to rotate from my hip and lift my side up. I was such an avid runner and I have always been active. It is hard to give that up. I often must walk with a cane now. I don't use it as often as I should because I am stubborn. I am a certified spinning instructor and I'm so passionate about it. I get on that bike and everything goes away. I still do it five or six times a week. But I refuse to use my cane walking into the gym. I would rather crawl into the building! I use it at the grocery store or when I know I'm going to be somewhere with uneven ground. I use it in church every weekend. I knew I needed a cane when I got to the point where I was hanging on my husband or my kids to keep from falling.

Don: I remember the day she got the cane. She got up early in the morning and went to the store. It took half an hour to pick out the perfect cane. But still, she left it in the corner of the room for a long time and never used it. I had to let Jenifer figure it out. I knew she'd do the right thing. But I am not going to tell her she can't do something. She is so strong-willed. If she falls she will get right back up. Still, it is hard to watch her struggle and I worry about her. Many of her friends try to treat her like an invalid. Jenifer is a very healthy and active person. She just walks with a limp. It does bother me to see her walk sometimes, or to get into bed and have to lift her leg up. The important thing is that I treat her with respect and that I wait until she really needs me to help her.

Jenifer was determined to lead her life as normally as she possibly could. Before she was diagnosed she rode in the MS Bike tour. Don would go up to watch her as she rode, raising money for MS even before she learned that she had the disease. After Jenifer was diagnosed, the couple and their children decided that they would participate in their local chapter's MS Walk as well.

Don: I told her that we needed to form a team. We would get as many friends and family involved as possible – Team Jenifer. We sent out emails and before you knew it we had almost two hundred people on our team! We are now the largest family team in the state of Connecticut and we've managed to pull in close to $300,000 in donations.

Through the MS Society the couple met another family who had been touched by Multiple Sclerosis. Tragically, the mother and her two daughters were murdered shortly after that meeting.

Don: We were sitting around thinking that we really wanted to do something positive in the face of such evil. We decided that we would do a fundraiser at which we would ask for donations and *release luminary bags in name of the victims. The first year we raised $132,000 for the MS Society. That's when we realized that we are very successful fundraisers.*

Because the horrible tragedy had happened in such a small town, nearly everybody wanted to do something to help. Jenifer and Don's idea was just what was needed to give the residents a purpose and a means of expressing their condolences. "Lights of Hope" is now an annual charity event.

Jenifer: That's what has surprised me the most - how many people really wanted to help and support us.

Jennifer is a social butterfly, but naturally, she has had to slow down. The couple has found that they don't go out as often as they used to and instead often opt to order in and enjoy an evening together. And Jenifer worries that someday she will end up in a wheelchair.

Don: I keep telling her that we will take one day at a time. My mother used that phrase whenever we faced something difficult in our family. We've prepared our home, making it accessible. Other than that there's nothing else we can really do. We take one day at a time and keep hoping that there will be a treatment developed that will help.

Jenifer: Don is fighting for this like he is the one responsible for finding a cure. It blows me away. There are times when I don't want to do it, but he goes and goes. He wants to raise the money.

He wants to save me and everyone else who suffers from this disease.

But Don is not the only one working tirelessly for a cure. Jenifer has been the model for promotional materials and ads, as well as spoken on radio programs and appeared in TV public service announcements in order to raise awareness. And when she needed the assistance she and Don had worked so hard to provide for others, it has been there for her too.

Don: When Jenifer had her last MRI and she had all these new lesions, we were shocked. We were concerned about the meds they wanted her to go on and what the lesions would mean. Jen emailed Lisa (the state's top MS chapter officer) that Friday night asking for support. We expected her to get back to us on Monday, but Saturday morning at 9 a.m. Lisa called the house. That was really impressive to us. It was great to see that she were so responsive and really cared.

While Multiple Sclerosis was not what either of them expected from life, it has proven to be the inspiration for some of their most admirable achievements, and more importantly, the powerful evidence of the strength and depth of their devotion to one another

Strategies For A Strong Marriage

How You Can Create Doses Of Devotion In Your Life

When John Lennon penned the lyrics for *All You Need Is Love*, he not only created an iconic song but a catch phrase that made its way into the collective conscience of a generation.

But is it true? Is love alone enough to overcome the challenges that couples often face in their relationships? The answer is of course, no - especially when chronic illness becomes part of the equation. It is simply asking far too much of love to expect that emotion alone will carry the two of you through the trials and issues that arise.

In fact it is that very emotion, that marvelous sensation that drew you together in the first place that can sometimes trip up even the most devoted couples. When a chronic illness like Multiple Sclerosis is diagnosed the relationship undergoes a series of changes and adjustments. Often the caregiver can experience a sense of hopelessness. He may feel trapped and tired of all of the drama that has suddenly entered his life. That pressure often equals, and occasionally even exceeds, the trauma his ill spouse is going through. If these feelings are allowed to fester, if a couple does not manage to establish a means of communicating with honesty and empathy, love itself often gets the blame.

A spouse may ask, "If I am feeling so unhappy, so frustrated with this situation, does that mean that I don't love this person as much as I thought I did?" Those vows about sickness and health can begin to feel like a prison sentence rather than a pledge. And sadly what often follows is, "It isn't the MS, I've just fallen out of love with you." Or worse yet, "I've fallen in love with someone else."

But the truth is when you start with love and then add an assortment of additional "tools" you quickly realize that, as was discussed in chapter two, the benefits of staying in the marriage extends to both partners. Keeping your marriage strong in the face of Multiple Sclerosis isn't just to prove that you were sincere when you recited your vows. A strong marriage will bring you a heightened sense of self-worth, a feeling that your purpose in life is greater than you imagined, and most of all, you will develop a much deeper understanding of what real love is and enjoy a greater bond with your partner than most "healthy" couples ever achieve. Of course neither of you would have ever chosen to invite Multiple Sclerosis into your marriage, but it can definitely be looked at as a "blurse" - a term coined to describe situations that sometimes prove to be both a blessing and a curse. Finding the blessing in the midst of the curse is where you will discover what you need to keep your marriage strong.

When a physician identifies the source of a patient's symptoms he or she will then begin to look for the means to cure or treat the problem. A woman with breast cancer may receive chemotherapy, radiation and surgery. But she might also take part in biofeedback, exercise programs and counseling sessions. In short, the doctor will use a number of resources in the course of her treatment.

In this chapter we will share with you some techniques that have been tested and proven by scores of successful couples. They are not rules to be followed to the letter, but simply suggestions that will help you to design your own unique method for strengthening your relationship. Every marriage is different. As you read the stories in this book you will see that each couple has developed their own unique means of managing the issues and complexities of life with Multiple Sclerosis.

Know Your Enemy!

When a doctor delivers the diagnosis of Multiple Sclerosis the two of you need to transform yourselves from marriage partners to a fearless, fighting team. *This is war!* The strongest couples are those who fight it side-by-side, the ones who see themselves as brave soldiers charging into battle, or sometimes even as two scared souls huddled together in a muddy trench. Either way, each knows the other has their back and that the enemy is out there in the dark. It is not within their relationship.

Nearly every couple we interviewed made a concerted effort to learn everything they could about their common enemy. Armed with data, fears became manageable. With a plan to handle setbacks and challenges, steps to control the chaos were put into effect. An arsenal of options and strategies was amassed.

Many of the couples we interviewed chose the role of fundraising heroes as a means of waging the battle. Others chose to work together to keep themselves updated on all the latest treatments and drug trials. When Multiple Sclerosis is viewed as an enemy that must be vanquished, the couples found that it was much easier to place the blame for frustrations on the illness and not on their partner.

A few spouses reported that their first reaction upon learning of their spouse's illness was to retreat. There are few things a man despises more than a problem for which he can see no solution. But refusing to confront the illness, to learn all about its origins, progression and treatment options simply produced a longer, more uncomfortable period of helplessness. Even when faced with sobering predictions, the care partners who pushed past their reluctance to delve into the tough truths about MS often discovered that the fear of the unknown had been a far greater burden to bear. When they realized that it was not a given that their spouse would become totally disabled, most reported that they experienced a greater sense of equanimity over the situation.

Says Jennifer Digmann, "It has to be both of you taking on the world. We call the disease Multiple Sclero-*us*. Dan is my partner in crime. I have to lean on him. Our advice is to learn as much as you can and be supportive of one another because you are both going through this together."

Build A Strong Army

Your neurologist is the most important member of your MS army. He or she is your General. However, after interviewing dozens of couples we discovered that very few remained with the neurologist who first diagnosed their MS. What one couple expects and needs from their physician can vary tremendously from what another wants. Are you a couple who expects your doctor to show empathy? Do you need him or her to take the time to discuss your feelings, as well as your physical problems? Do you want your doctor to set aside time to answer each and every question that you have or are you just as happy to be given reading materials for your own research? Or perhaps the two of you want a hard driving type of neurologist who is on top of all of the newest treatment options - a no nonsense, straight-forward type who expects you to handle the emotional issues on your own. Deciding what you would like to accomplish during medical appointments and what each of you would like to discuss is an important exercise to go through before you enter your doctor's office. If you find that your neurologist is not meeting your needs, move on. This is the General who is to command the charge into battle. You don't want to follow a leader in whom you have little or no faith.

Family and friends can be a very important part of your MS army. Or not. Many of our interviewees have discovered that MS can often cause people to pull away. Sometimes people don't know what to do or say so they simply make themselves scarce. When this behavior is demonstrated by close family members it is particularly difficult to accept. But realizing that not every soldier must sign up in the first week will help you to allow these reluctant warriors time to process their fears and misgivings. Or perhaps to reveal the sad truth that some friends weren't actually friends at all.

Says Marty Kuchar, "MS weeds out the people who you don't need in your life. We've had great support from family and friends. But some people have faded away from us. Now we know who we can rely on."

The most successful marriages have found a means to induct many friends and family members into their army, and in turn, have extended to these people a way to feel useful. Several of the couples interviewed have developed massive Walk MS and Bike MS teams and raised tens of thousands of dollars in the process. As Jenifer Walsh reports, "Don is fighting for this like he is the one responsible for finding a cure. It blows me away. There are times that I don't want to do it, but he goes and goes. He wants to raise the money. He wants to save me and everyone else who suffers from this disease."

Accept Your New Reality

It is inevitable that both of you will sometimes experience moments of longing for the days before Multiple Sclerosis became a part of your world. Photos of you hiking mountain trails together or playing on a company softball team can bring up memories of a time

45

that seemed so much less complicated. But was it? Your new reality may include mobility tools and daily injections, but it can still be a life filled with laughter, adventure and most of all, love. Movie nights on the couch together with a favorite snack or a great bottle of wine are a fantastic way of connecting, of feeling close and sharing something you both enjoy.

One couple we interviewed has become passionate about jigsaw puzzles. They've always got one at some stage of completion. As she told us, "He sometimes calls me from work to suggest a way to solve a particularly difficult puzzle and we'll strategize over the phone. I know it sounds a little silly, but it is an obsession we share. Before I became ill, we were both so caught up in our careers we could have never imagined the joy we'd get from such a simple and quirky task as assembling jigsaw puzzles! We are truly closer now that we have ever been."

Perhaps the most significant and positive change that can result from the limitations that Multiple Sclerosis brings to your life is a greater appreciation for those quiet moments, the days when you just simply enjoy one another's company. Many couples reported that for the first time in their marriage they were sharing their thoughts in a truly intimate manner. The closeness that developed between them extended far beyond the love they once thought was as strong as it could ever be.

Reports Suzanne Pershall, "Everyone is so busy running and rushing, and when I couldn't do that anymore it made me really reflect on what was important in my life. Now I love just sitting next to Richard on the sofa and enjoying his company. It's not about having the best things or the newest things. It is wonderful to just slow down and really enjoy life."

Life comes to an end for all of us. It is how we value our years on earth that matters. Couples in strong marriages have learned to savor their time together. They have come to appreciate that the purest expression of their devotion can be something as simple as a tender word of affection, spoken when their partner is struggling with the fear and uncertainty of chronic illness.

Couples living with Multiple Sclerosis know that time is precious, nothing in life is guaranteed and while love may not cure all, it can certainly soften some of the blows.

Talk...And Then Talk Some More

All successful couples report that open and honest communication is important to the health and happiness of their marriage. When chronic illness becomes a part of the marriage these skills become absolutely essential. Giving one another a safe place in which to discuss the frustrations and fears that each of you are experiencing is a way of defusing their power to undermine confidence and joy. These difficult conversations are the very building blocks of a strong marriage. The honesty expressed is what ultimately draws you closer together.

In marriages where illness is not (yet!) a factor there is seldom a need to inform your spouse about the inner workings of your body, your fatigue level or the scale of your pain. Couples who successfully navigate the unpredictable waters of chronic illness are pros at communicating their symptoms honestly and succinctly. The key is to understand when and how much to share. A constant stream of complaints will eventually become no more than annoying background noise in any marriage.

Some good indications of whether or not you should discuss a symptom with your spouse are as follows:

1. **The symptom you are experiencing is an entirely new one for you**. This is indicative of an MS attack rather than a flare-up or exacerbation. Attacks often require medical attention, or at the very least, need to be reported to your physician. This is definitely not the time to be stoic.

2. **The problem is becoming too difficult for you to handle on your own.** Pain is an issue for many MS patients. The day-to-day discomfort that you may live with is not something that generally needs to be

discussed with your spouse - at least not on a day-to-day basis! But searing, debilitating pain is something no one should suffer alone. Tell your partner when your pain reaches this level. You may need medical intervention. Even if there is not an immediate solution for your pain, the reassurance that a loved one can provide is invaluable. The most important question that your spouse should ask you in this situation is, "Do you need me to get help for you or do you just need me to provide comfort for you?"

3. **You've reached your physical limit**. It is perfectly reasonable to tell your partner that you need to stop and rest for a while. Anyone who has suffered with Multiple Sclerosis for some time knows that there is no way to simply power through fatigue or muscle weakness. However, you lose credibility with your spouse and loved ones if you never make an effort to participate in activities. It is time to look at mobility devices if you truly cannot manage to walk a short distance. There is also a medication that might help you walk better. Discuss this option with your doctor. Always be honest about your limitations and communicate them with a clear voice.

4. **Your sadness has become a burden too great to bear alone**. We all mourn the loss of our former selves. There is a constant emotional toll to be paid as Multiple Sclerosis slowly takes more away from us. Medication

can help. Often your doctor will prescribe anti-depressants. But there is seldom anything more soothing than the tender words of someone who loves you. Ask for them when they are sincerely needed. At times just hearing "I'm so sorry that this is happening to you" can make the sorrow a bit more bearable. As Rebecca Kucher says of her husband Marty, "He is my calming spirit and my perfect balance. I'm a little high-strung and always go to the negative. He has kept me above the fold."

Understanding the worth of honest communication in a strong marriage is crucial, but recognizing the importance of timing is just as essential. As a spouse is at the front door, exhausted from a day at the office, the words "We need to talk" are rarely met with enthusiasm. "I've been struggling more than usual today with my MS, can you let me know when you are available to dispense a few of your healing words?" is much more likely to produce the empathy and consideration you seek.

For some people, clear and concise communication comes easy to them. For others, however, it is far more difficult to express their feelings, particularly when those feelings consist of fear, longing, and despair.

Many people who suffer from Multiple Sclerosis have reported that they were afraid that if they were honest about their feelings, if they expressed exactly what they were thinking, it would place too great a burden on their spouse. "If he can't solve the problem, why should I share it with him?" was one response we heard from a woman who was struggling in her marriage.

But what these people don't realize is that they are communicating. Just not with their words. The long silences, the deep sighs and the expressions of pain etched on their faces often speak so much more piercingly then they realize. More importantly, it left their spouse feeling powerless and confused. In strong marriages both partners are adept at voicing their needs, but also at reading the "silent messages" and encouraging open communication.

Spouses who cultivate an acute degree of perceptiveness towards their partners fluctuating symptoms and react in a calming and helpful manner create an environment of sympathy and compassion that promotes both emotional, as well as physical healing. That intuitive behavior, the manner in which spouses in strong marriages manage to focus in on their partner's moods, plays a tremendous role in the health of the relationship.
It is extremely important, however, that compassion and understanding is a two way street. The strongest marriages are ones in which there is a nearly equal level of consideration between both the chronically ill member and the healthy partner.

Guard Her Heart, Not Just Her Health

Be an advocate for your partner's well-being, a vital collaborator in medical decisions and a fearless fellow warrior in the battle against Multiple Sclerosis. But never fall into the role of the Pill Police.

Reported one woman, "At times I feel like I am alone with my misery. He thinks that if he reads articles on new treatments and lectures me about how so and so is running marathons, he's doing his part. All he is doing is making me feel like a failure as a MS patient."

It is important to keep abreast of the latest developments in MS research. Fortunately, there are so many new treatments being developed. But until a cure is found, medicine alone can only do so much. It is the nurturing attention that only you, her loving spouse, can give that will provide the fortitude she needs for the battle she's fighting.

Bill Jackson is an excellent example of a man who found the perfect balance between being a diligent guardian of his wife's well-being, as well as her knight in shining armor. "Even when she went into a nursing home, I would go there every day from eight in the morning to five at night. And if she called me at three in the morning, I'd go back. I made sure that she had fresh flowers in her room every day."

52

Divide & Conquer!

Being honest about your abilities, or lack of, is extremely important for the smooth operation of the household. However, if a couple has based their relationship on traditional gender-specific roles the transition into new positions of responsibility can be challenging. Often times a husband or wife can feel overwhelmed by the demands of being both a provider and a caretaker. Add in dishes, laundry, dusting, grocery shopping, and vacuuming and you've got the recipe for a serious burn-out. If you are raising children as well, the responsibilities can seem almost unbearable.

When a husband becomes ill his wife may experience an entirely different set of disappointments and frustrations. If she has held the primary position of caregiver and household manager for the family, and now must also take on the role of primary breadwinner, the load can be overwhelming. When MS strikes her spouse just as her children are leaving the nest, her own long-held dreams of freedom and new opportunities may be dashed. If these issues are not addressed a new kind of weariness and discontent can over-shadow her love and affection for her husband.

Recognizing the pressures that MS puts on the healthy spouse and taking steps to alleviate the burdens that they must bear is essential for the survival of the partnership. If finances allow, a weekly visit by a housekeeper can be godsend. Or enlist the help of your support team for reinforcements. One couple sings the praises of a particularly thoughtful friend who always organizes a group of neighbors to deliver weekly casseroles when times are tough.

But sometimes even the most loving partner needs a little break from all of the drama. Just as important as providing care for your spouse is giving yourself permission to get away. This is a perfect time to call on your support army. Ask a friend to stay with your spouse while you grab a few days of golf or fishing or just being by yourself.

As Lynn Forrette says of her husband, Mark, "Many times he's too tired to go out in the evening or there are too many stairs. And then I am torn. I feel guilty going without him. If it's something I really want to do, I still go. If it's something that doesn't really matter, I stay home."

Learning your limitations and lovingly communicating your frustrations is just as important, maybe even more so, for a caregiver to as it is for a spouse who is struggling with chronic illness.

Become Affection Aficionados

Any long-married couple will attest to the fact that intimacy changes as the anniversaries accumulate. In the best of relationships it matures into a deeper, more meaningful bond. But that transformation is not a given. It often requires a series of subtle modifications and an acceptance of the fact that you no longer possess the energy or the libido that you had at twenty-two. Most of all, it often requires discovering additional ways of expressing the passion that you still have for one another. Sex does not necessarily become a thing of the past when Multiple Sclerosis is a factor though. Many issues can be solved by discussing any problems you may be experiencing with your physician.

When chronic illness enters a marriage it sometimes becomes necessary to develop new ways of keeping the romance alive. But as every couple in a strong marriage reports, the journey to a new means of loving one another can produce an even greater level of satisfaction with the physical aspect of their relationship. The couples who have been the most successful at making this transformation do so by taking the time to enjoy the pleasure of one another's touch. It can be as simple as holding hands on the couch. Or as personal as bathing one another.

As Julie Hare related, "Now we take showers together and he washes me. It is the sweetest, most intimate thing."

But accepting the new realities of life with Multiple Sclerosis does not necessarily mean that a couple needs to abandon all of the ways that they once enjoyed each other. As Jeanne and Chip Allen discovered, their love of slow dancing needn't be a thing of the past. It just needed a little adjustment.

There is no better definition of true love than the way Dave Rice treats his wife, Marty. As she reports, "He does incredibly personal stuff for me and yet he still kisses me like he really loves me. Kissing the person that I am and forgetting about having to take care of the package that I am in."

Steve & Julie Hare

❧

Often times life hinges on a twist of fate. If it had been a typical sunny day on the beach in Santa Cruz, CA Steve and Julie Hare might not have ever fallen in love. If Julie and her girlfriend hadn't encountered a foggy morning at the coast, they would not have cancelled their beach plans and returned to a friend's house that they had stopped at along the way. It was at that house that Julie had first laid eyes on a handsome, long-haired guy in a t-shirt and shorts who was sitting on the couch swirling a glass of wine. She didn't realize that he had also taken note of her. Not surprising, considering she was a vibrant, pretty nineteen year old who was playfully dressed for a day in the sun.

Julie: I was wearing a tank top and shorts.

Steve: That tank top really caught my eye!

They ended up talking all night long and found they shared many interests. A few weeks later they went on a camping trip and just three months after that they were living together. In 1983 they were married. As two quintessential California kids, they looked forward to a life of hiking, kayaking and enjoying the adventures that beach living had to offer. Steve began a career in the wine business and Julie became a teacher. A few years later, they welcomed their two daughters, Kristen and Lily.

In 2003, however, a scarcely recognizable omen of misfortune appeared. The strange sensation of numbness and hyper-sensitivity that had developed in Julie's left arm and shoulder hardly seemed cause for alarm though. Her left hip also just felt wrong in some strange and hard to explain manner. Her gait even changed slightly. Most disturbingly, she noticed it was becoming more and more difficult to keep up with her fellow teachers as they chased after the children in their charge. But none of these minor changes seemed like something that needed to be viewed as distressing and requiring immediate attention. After all, she had a family, a career and an active life. No wonder she occasionally felt a little tired. But a nagging voice in the back of Julie's head told her that this was more than just the garden variety aches and pains of a busy, young teacher.

Julie: I tried to put it out of my mind but gradually it was getting harder and harder to walk. I went to the doctor and he suggested that we just keep an eye on things. The term Multiple Sclerosis was only mentioned. Even though I knew very little about that disease, something told me that's exactly what I had. Of course, I never voiced those concerns. But the fear, the uncertainty of what was happening was taking its toll on me.

Although Julie attempted to deny what was happening, one night the frustration that came with trying to communicate those underlying fears with Steve caused Julie to reach a breaking point.

Julie: We had just made dinner and I was standing with a plate of food in my hand. I don't know what came over me but suddenly the anger, frustration and fear bubbled up. I needed him to pay attention. I threw my plate on the floor, and then picked up another plate and threw it on the floor as well! The act was so unlike me.

Steve: That certainly caught my attention! We don't usually hold a lot back from each other verbally but somehow we just couldn't bring ourselves to face what was in front of us.

In spite of that dramatic display of Julie's growing concerns they both would attempt to stay in this state of denial for six more years before finally, in 2009, Julie and Steve sought another opinion. Her symptoms had continued to worsen and it just was no longer possible to pretend that nothing was seriously wrong. After an MRI, a lumbar puncture and various other tests, Julie's early suspicion was confirmed with a definitive diagnosis of Multiple Sclerosis. Now they were forced to face the fact that life as they knew it was about to change.

Steve: It was surreal. I just kept thinking this isn't happening. She's going to wake up tomorrow and be fine. I buried my head in the sand. In retrospect, after Julie told me, I should have started looking for more information. I hadn't ever been around sickness in my life. I'm an only child and I have been incredibly healthy. Even my parents were healthy until they passed. I really had never been around anyone who was chronically ill. I was in no way prepared for this.

Julie: In a way I was relieved to finally have an answer for my puzzling symptoms. Now there was an explanation and it was a vindication of sorts. That's not to say I wasn't afraid of MS, but I did not imagine myself in a wheelchair. I am a very physical person, and I certainly feared losing that, but I still believed that the disease wouldn't change me. That may have simply been my way of denying the reality of my situation.

News such as this can raise doubts for any couple as to whether or not they can cope with what lies ahead. For Julie and Steve, however, there was no doubt about whether or not they would face the future together.

> *Ultimately, we both had a choice. It is a choice to stay together that we made without hesitation…and we continue to make every day.*

Steve: At first I wasn't sure I could handle it. I still don't know if I can handle it. I just do my best. I realize it's a lot harder for her. She's living with this. If I could wave a magic wand and take it from her I would. I didn't sign up for MS when I got married, but I did sign up for Julie. I've honestly never had any thoughts of leaving when I learned of her illness. There were times before the diagnosis when I thought of walking out, particularly when we had two cantankerous teenage girls in the house. But when MS came into our life I never had any doubt that we would stay together.

Julie: Oh my God, that's so true. Ultimately, we both had a choice. It is a choice to stay together that we made without hesitation…and we continue to make every day.

Julie is a very private person by nature. She is someone who doesn't share her emotions easily with the world. A slight-built, rather reserved woman, Julie at first glance seems more fragile than she actually is. But there is a strength and determination about her that is clearly evident when she speaks. An intelligent, thoughtful woman, she expresses herself with honesty and candor. Julie is definitely not a victim of Multiple Sclerosis, but in the early days the disease caused her to withdraw even more from others.

Julie: I really pulled myself into an emotional cave. I didn't want anyone to see me having difficulty walking. I had tried to hide it for so long. Suddenly I was overwhelmed by my emotions. In retrospect, I wish I wouldn't have been so humiliated by it. I wish I would have reached out and shared more.

Initially Julie was diagnosed with Relapsing Remitting Multiple Sclerosis, but that diagnosis was quickly changed to Secondary Progressive MS, and the realities of living with a degenerative disease soon became apparent to each of them.

Julie: So many things are different in my life. The simplest things have changed. Now everything is an event and nothing is spontaneous. Every time I leave the house I need to consider what I will have to bring with me in order to navigate the world out there.

Steve: Julie is much more patient than I ever knew she was, and much more resilient.

His once long brown hair is now a striking shade of silver and neatly trimmed, but barefoot and clad in a

Hawaiian print shirt and shorts, the carefree, young California boy is still obviously present in Steve. With a twinkle in his eyes, he's undeniably a charming and compassionate man who greets everyone with a heart-felt bear hug. Being in the hospitality industry as a tasting room manager, he has a natural affinity for people and an easy, relaxed congeniality that causes nearly everyone who meets him to feel as though they've just found a new friend. His agreeable nature, however, has been severely tested by Multiple Sclerosis.

Steve: I do get frustrated and she knows it. I can even get to the point where I say, "I f**king hate MS." And I admit that I sometimes mourn the loss of my individual life. These days my life is basically three things; work, taking care of Julie and running my wine business. I miss being able to take my kayak out. I miss having a partner to hike with and I often miss my dream of what our life was supposed to be.

But in spite of his frustrations, Steve recognizes that his role as Julie's support partner is one that he willingly accepts with grace and commitment. It was not the role he wanted in her life. It is not the future he expected the two of them would share. But it is a duty that he sees as perhaps the most sacred of vows between them. And he knows, beyond the shadow of doubt, that she would do the same for him if their positions had been reversed.

Julie: Steve has helped me so much. He really hangs in there. He is one of the most nurturing people I have ever met. I didn't know that about him before. Through this experience, however, I have really learned gratitude. I don't think I even knew what it was before. I've learned to be thankful for even the most simple of pleasures, to live in the moment. And I have a much greater appreciation of Steve. I think I took him for granted before. Amazingly, I think he loves me even more now.

But while emotional love may deepen, the physical expression of that love is often changed by a diagnosis of Multiple Sclerosis. As mobility issues increase in severity and painful spasms make it difficult to create an atmosphere of romance, often times the old ways of expressing desire are replaced with new and even more passionate demonstrations of love.

Steve: I have learned a much broader definition of the word love. We are intimate in a much deeper way now. As far as sex goes, she has limited movement and I have a mental image of hurting her. But I love the way we cuddle and I honestly love the closeness that we have now.

Julie: It has definitely affected our sex life and that bothers me. But now we hold hands more, and kiss, and touch. Now we take showers together and he washes me. It is the sweetest, most intimate thing.

This newfound intimacy and closeness that MS brought into their lives would prove to be essential in helping them navigate their way through the additional challenges that they would soon be forced to face. Steve was to learn that his job was ending. And it was clear that Julie would never return to her career as an educator. With their financial concerns pressing on them, one night in November they attended an MS support group. Ironically the topic of the night was thankfulness. As people in various stages of the disease around the room expressed all of the things that they were grateful for, Steve and Julie were forced to examine their own life.

Steve: All I could think about was how I was out of a job. And then I started thinking, how narrow-minded of me to think that way. I am one of the only people in this room without MS and here I am focusing on this crap.

On the way home Julie was reflecting on all of the support that had been provided to them. She suggested that not only was it something they could be thankful for, but maybe they should try to find a way to return the favor. Maybe it was time to stop feeling sorry for themselves. When they arrived home a photograph that they had looked at a thousand times suddenly took on new meaning. It was an old black and white picture of Steve's grandparents. His grandmother was looking adoringly on as his grandfather, equipped with boxing gloves, stood in a playful stance. The idea came to Steve in a flash. That photo would make the perfect wine label.

That one little revelation would change their lives.

Dipping into their courage and their 401K, Julie and Steve created Counter Punch Wines. It would give them a purpose in life, a passion they could share and a means of giving back. They would donate a portion of the proceeds from their wine sales to help find a cure. Suddenly the disease that they thought would rob them of their dreams had become the very inspiration they need to launch them into an exciting new enterprise that they would create together.

Steve: We started Counter Punch Wines with the mutual goals of generating funds that would allow us to give something back to organizations that help "counter punch" the effects of MS, while producing small lots of great wines from California's best vineyards.

Julie: I remember that night so well. He was looking at that photograph and grinning broadly. I got a warm feeling that told me something wonderful was about to happen. It had been a very long time since I had seen him so enthusiastic. I suddenly realized that sharing a venture that we would be passionate about, and that somehow felt larger than either of us, would give us another avenue in which to share our lives with one another.

Steve had been in the wine industry for a long time and knew all the ins and outs of marketing wine. In just a matter of months Counter Punch Wines became a successful business and a turning point in their journey with Multiple Sclerosis. They now produce an outstanding Merlot and a Cabernet Sauvignon, as well as two Chardonnays from different vineyard designations.

Together they began pouring their wine at MS functions and wine tasting events. It wasn't long before Julie became so caught up in the fun and exhilaration of their adventure that those old feelings of humiliation and the need to hide her disease disappeared. She has become a fixture at wine events with her trademark carved wooden walking stick and her warm and welcoming smile.

Julie: I would advise anyone diagnosed with this disease to reach out to others and take advantage of the help that is available. Don't hold back. You are not alone. Most importantly, don't isolate yourself. I remember one night I was attending a meeting and the question was posed, "What do we value most in our society?" The answer that most of the people gave was "independence", but the moderator asked us what if we valued "interdependence"? I could accept help from Steve but had found it difficult to be accepting of help from others. MS has made me become a kinder, more generous person who can give as well as accept kindness and generosity from others. I'm a much better person than I was before I got MS.

From his perch on a chair next to Julie, Steve seems lost in thought and clearly moved by her words.

Steve: Maybe I am too.

Turning to look at him and holding him in a strong and determined gaze, she answers that question without hesitation.

Julie: Without a doubt you are!

Suzanne & Richard Pershall

"When we get up in the morning, he can look in my eyes and pretty much tell what kind of day I am going to have."

You can only hope to end up with a spouse like Richard, someone who has such a deep understanding and knowledge of his wife that all he has to do is look in her eyes to know what she needs from him.

Perhaps that is because Suzanne and Richard were good friends for many years before they were a couple. They met in 1979 while both were married to other people. The two couples lived in the same apartment complex and spent time together playing cards and going dancing. They were even present at the hospital when each other's children were born. After both of them divorced their respective partners, the two stayed in contact via Christmas cards and an occasional holiday get-together.

Richard was living in Lafayette and Suzanne had relocated to Shreveport. One day Richard came across a photo of Suzanne and, for some reason, decided that he needed to talk to her.

Richard: I was sitting in my office going through a box of old pictures. I ran across a photo from Christmas one year. It was of Suzanne sitting on the floor with my son. I looked at the picture and thought I really need to call her.

Suzanne: Richard called me at work. When they told me who it was I thought something awful had happened. I answered by asking him what was wrong. I was relieved to hear everything was okay. After that day we started talking on the phone on a regular basis. Then he and the kids came to visit.

The conversations and visits became more regular. The transition to a couple was a smooth and seemingly natural one for the two friends. They each believed that this was their second chance at happiness.

Richard: It was September of 1991 when I started making trips back and forth. By the time we got through the holidays we were dating regularly on the weekends. We were just good friends to start with. We felt the same way about a lot of things. She was the kind of person I could be friends with after my divorce. That was the intent to start with, then we got to where we were best friends. I could talk to her about anything that was going on. I'll admit it didn't hurt that she was drop-dead gorgeous too. Before long I knew I was in love with her.

Suzanne: After that first phone call it was pretty much the same way for me. I think over the next couple of months, just talking on the phone with him, I knew I was already falling in love. I always thought he was a really great person. He was great to his last wife and to his kids.

After a year and many miles racked up between the two cities, it was Richard and Suzanne's children who gave their parents the push they needed to take the plunge into marriage.

Suzanne: Our kids said that they were tired of traveling back and forth. They didn't understand why we didn't get married.

On Dec 5th of 1992, that is precisely what they did. Amongst family and loved ones at a friend's house in Shreveport they said their vows and began their life together. From the very beginning, Richard revealed himself as a hopeless romantic.

Richard: Before we got married I promised her our life together would never be boring. I would see to that personally. I think she'll tell you that I have kept that promise. I've always felt that when you begin a relationship with someone you, you should never start anything that you cannot continue to do for the rest of your life. In other words, when we were dating I would send her flowers out of the blue for no reason and I still do that twenty-two years later.

There are a lot of things that the sight of a beautiful bouquet of flowers can remedy, but four years into their marriage they would see the first signs of something that couldn't be mended by flowers or romantic gestures.

Suzanne had her twenty year class reunion coming up, and like most women, she had ten pesky pounds that she wanted to rid herself of so that she could fit into a dress that she loved. She teamed up with a piece of exercise equipment similar to a rowing machine and was diligent about using it every morning. Her hard work paid off and she made it to her reunion in her perfect dress on the arm of her loving husband. She had noticed, however, that there was something different about holding his hand.

Suzanne: My right hand was really bothering me. This piece of exercise equipment caused me to use my hands a lot and I also used the computer on a regular basis. When I noticed my hand was going numb I thought I was getting carpal tunnel. Driving back after the reunion, I fell asleep and when I woke up I noticed that the back of my neck hurt. I got up Monday morning and kept up with the health rider and my usual routine, trying to ignore the symptoms I was experiencing. By Friday morning the whole right side of my face was numb, plus the numbness in my hand had was still present. Around ten or eleven o'clock I noticed that the numbness had spread down my arm and body. I told the doctor I work with what was going on. By the time we were done with our conversation it had spread all the way down my body. He thought I was having a stroke and sent me over for an MRI. After the test I went back to the office, packed my stuff and headed home. Just a little while later the doctor called me and said that he talked to the radiologist. He assured me that I didn't have a stroke but explained that he had seen white matter on my brain. He mentioned a few things it might be and MS was one of them. He told me to just take it easy that weekend, relax and don't stress out. He said he was going to make an appointment with a neurologist for me on Monday morning.

As is so often the case, Suzanne wouldn't get an immediate explanation for her symptoms. She went to the neurologist, who again said that MS was a possibility, but he wanted her to see a specialist. The family had a camping trip planned for the week and Suzanne had no intention of letting a possible diagnosis of any sort ruin it. The neurologist told her that they would get her in to see the specialist when she returned. She thought that some time away with her family would do her good and would probably alleviate some of the symptoms she was experiencing. As it would turn out, over the course of the next several days, she would become more certain than ever that something was terribly wrong.

Suzanne: The numbness got worse. I couldn't pick up anything. I was dropping everything and I was exhausted. I pretty much stayed in the camper the whole time we were there. We got back and I told the neurologist everything that happened. He got me an appointment with an MS specialist.

Initially the neurologist suggested that they try and alleviate the symptoms with steroids and then wait to see if they flared up again. But Richard was having no part in sitting idly by, waiting for his wife's health to decline any further. He was adamant that they make the appointment with the specialist immediately. Suzanne was grateful to have him there by her side to speak up, but to her the appointment seemed like a mere formality. There was a small voice inside her head telling her that Multiple Sclerosis was the cause of her problems.

Suzanne: When my doctor called me that first afternoon and said it was possible that it was Multiple Sclerosis, I was shocked. I seriously thought that I had had a stroke. And then, the more I thought about it, I realized "Oh my gosh, I bet that's what it is." We went on the internet and read about the disease. I think from that day on I knew that's what it was. To me it was the only logical explanation, especially with the fatigue.

They went to their appointment with the MS specialist and within fifteen minutes Suzanne received her official diagnosis. Although Suzanne had already known and accepted that this was going to be the answer, Richard was surprised.

Richard: At first you feel shocked and sad for her. As much as anything just because of the unknown. I started doing research. When you go online and start doing that the sources seem to sensationalize everything. What you read about are all of the worst cases. We know there are a lot of people who have progressive MS who really suffer and the disease progresses rapidly. What you don't understand initially is that there are a lot of people who do better.

It's not uncommon to wonder what your significant other's response would be to that kind of news. You wonder what they will do when the chips are down. Richard proved his love to be steadfast and unwavering. It was clear from the very beginning that his concern would not be for himself or what he would have to endure, but only for his wife and how it would affect her.

Richard: I wasn't afraid about how I was going to handle it. That never entered my mind. I was just afraid for her. We're a very active couple. I didn't know how difficult it would be for her to cope if we were no longer able to enjoy the lifestyle we both loved.

Along with being able to rely on her husband, Suzanne also had her faith. Her mother, who was living with them at the time, was also able to help guide her through the uncertain and difficult times.

Suzanne: I was afraid of how things would transpire as the disease went along but my mother was a wonderful person and she taught my brother and me that with God all things are possible. No matter what, no matter how we feel about a situation, we can get through anything as long as we believe we can do it. Anything is possible.

There are a lot of unknowns that swirl around a diagnosis of Multiple Sclerosis. No one can be assured as to how the disease will affect them, what symptoms they will have, or how quickly it will progress. There are no answers as to why you got it in the first place, or even what might be the best treatment for you. Those are usually the most frightening aspects for people, but for Suzanne it was something with which she was painful familiar that brought her to tears on the way home from her appointment.

Suzanne: My father was diabetic and seeing him give himself shots was always terribly frightening to me. The thought of having to give myself one every day scared me to death. We got in the car to drive home and I began crying, just boo hoo-ing. Richard somehow knew exactly why. He grabbed my hand and said, "When I was a little boy I didn't want to brush my teeth. At first my mom tried to help me but I needed to do it on my own so my mom and dad kept after me. They would tell me I had to do it or my teeth were going to fall out. We'll take the same attitude. I will be with you every time. We'll do it because we have to and because it's going to keep you well."

Three of their children were living with them at the time. They were all teens or about to enter those problematic years and the couple was not certain how this news would be received. They needn't have worried. Suzanne soon discovered that she had yet another devoted cheering section.

We'll take whatever comes and do our best. Happiness is a choice.

Suzanne: While we were on vacation they knew something was wrong because I wasn't doing anything. Then we got back home and I saw the specialist. We went home that night and sat them down. We try not to ever lie to our children about anything. We told them what Multiple Sclerosis was and we showed them pamphlets from the doctor. I think it scared the eleven year old the most. They all asked if I was going to die from it. That was the first question. We told them that I wasn't going to die and I think they did very well with it after that. Soon after - I will never forget this - we took them to see Phantom of the Opera. We were sitting in the balcony level. When the performance was over there were so many people trying to get on the elevator. My balance wasn't the best, so both of my kids got on each side of me and said "Come on mom, we will carry you if we need to."

In fact, according to Richard, Suzanne's illness has provided the children with an incredibly valuable set of life lessons.

Richard: I think they have gone through an evolution. Initially they were in a bit of denial, just because of a lack of education, and as we went along and kept teaching them they got out of that phase. The way that we've handled it and how well Suzanne has done, I think it's made them all stronger. What we've done is taken lemons and made lemonade. We have a great life and we've never expected anything else. We'll take whatever comes and do our best. Happiness is a choice.

Suzanne: They can tell if I'm getting tired and I need to rest; especially my daughter. They have never been negative or embarrassed about it. They tell their friends. I think it's important for people to see how well I have done.

Even when you make the choice to be happy there are bound to be moments of sorrow. Suzanne's mother provided her with some tough love during those times.

Suzanne: I would have my pity parties. My mom would give me about thirty minutes, and then she would tell me I needed to be done. That's how we've always lived.

There are very few areas of your life that this disease doesn't manage effect in some manner. It scoffs in the face of plans and sweeps everything you thought you knew about your world right out from underneath you, forcing you to become a master at adapting and improvising. One of the first changes that Suzanne had to make was in her career.

Suzanne: I had to leave my position because I never got the feeling back in my right hand up to my elbow. It was hard for me to draw syringes and take blood pressures. I stayed with it for a couple years and then I just couldn't do it anymore. I moved into the business office and started doing all the medical billing. In 2005 our last child was graduating from high school so I retired. I haven't worked since then. Now I just get to enjoy taking care of Richard and our home.

Richard: I'm a full time job!

With the children out of the house and Suzanne retired from her job, the couple found time to dedicate themselves to helping find a cure for Multiple Sclerosis by volunteering at events and at the offices of the National MS Society.

Richard: I started in Houston doing the MS 150 bike ride. In Denver I did the motorcycle ride. I started it because I felt like it was the only way I could contribute to finding a cure. That was my motivation. When we moved here I bought a motorcycle and I got involved with the MS 150 Gold Wings. I did that for a couple of years when the guy who was heading up that group asked me if I would take it over. I agreed, so I have been on the core committee for the MS 150 for five years. I'm in charge of the motorcycle escort group. Now I'm a virtual rider. I can raise money just like I was doing before. I have raised a pretty decent amount - twenty-one thousand dollars two years ago and fifty-one thousand last year.

Suzanne: The first couple years I rode on the motorcycle with him. But it became more difficult getting on and off the motorcycle so the volunteer coordinator asked me if I would like to be her assistant. I started volunteering in the office, doing things to help her with the Walk MS, Bike MS and Hike MS events. We have luncheons in the business community and I am also an ambassador for the Colorado chapter. I work for the National MS Society information resource center. I am there to help the coordinator with whatever she needs done.

Those events got the couple out and socializing with others who were going through a lot of the same trials and tribulations that they were. They both found the work to be incredibly rewarding.

Suzanne: Connections make a difference. People don't need to feel like they are on their own. There are so many of us and we all have something to offer and something to share.

As they became accustomed to the limitations of Suzanne's illness they were able to make the necessary adjustments that enabled them to do many of the things they had always enjoyed.

Richard: We structure our social life around how she feels. We take ballroom dancing lessons. It's something we enjoy doing but we let her health dictate our schedule. If she is feeling good we go out, if she's not we stay home.

Suzanne: I never feel guilty about being sick because he has never made me feel like that. He's the first one to say "Let's get back into bed" or "Let's just lounge around on the couch and watch movies or something." I don't even have to say anything.

For someone who was a caretaker by nature, as well as professionally, it was a difficult task for Suzanne to transition into the role of the one who needed care.

Suzanne: It was tough for me in the beginning because I was raised to be very independent. I have always been in the medical field so I have always been the caregiver. It was very hard. I wanted to be able to have my life continue exactly the way it had been going. The first four years I was in and out of the hospital. Over the years, with Richard's help and our children's help, I finally realized that I can't do it all and that I have to ask for assistance. Now I don't even hesitate. If I feel like it's something that I need help with I am the first one to ask for it. But in the beginning it was super hard to do that.

Part of that transformation was the realization that asking for help and accepting it didn't make her weak but actually just served as yet another demonstration of how resilient she actually was.

Richard: I already knew she was a strong person, otherwise we would have never gotten married. Some of the things that have made me really proud are the way that she shows others how to handle MS in a positive way. My workplace is a small office. Three years ago one of the young ladies who worked there was diagnosed with Multiple Sclerosis. She had just gotten married and wanted to have children. She and her husband had a ton of questions. The positive influence that Suzanne had on her was huge. For them to see Suzanne and how well she was doing was very reassuring. Multiple Sclerosis doesn't always create severe limitations.

Suzanne: Everyone has been very supportive. What my family gives to me, what support I live with…I want to pass that on to other people who are suffering more than I am.

Suzanne is able to find positive ways that her illness has affected her as well.

Suzanne: I worked at the clinic for thirteen years and also had a job at my church. We have always been a very active, busy couple. I think that MS slows me down and makes me look at life in a different way. Everyone is so busy running and rushing, and when I couldn't do that anymore it made me really reflect on what was important in my life. Now I love just sitting next to Richard on the sofa and enjoying his company. It's not about having the best things or the newest things. It is wonderful to just slow down and really enjoy life.

Enjoying her life involves spending time with the man of her dreams, the man who vowed to continue to keep her life interesting and to demonstrate his love for her with grand romantic gestures.

Richard: I work on old cars as a hobby and I had been spending a lot of time in the garage. One Friday afternoon I sent her an email and told her that she should have the dogs taken care of and get some evening attire. A car would pick her up at 5:30. I went and bought new clothes that she wasn't used to seeing me in. I had a limo driver pick us up and we took her to a restaurant that's one of her favorites. We had ordered appetizers and a bottle of wine when I reached in my pocket and pulled out a box. I told her, "This is for your patience with me working on the car so much." It was diamond earrings. She went nuts. Then I reached in the other pocket and said, "This is just because I love you as much as I do." It was the necklace to match. I had a dozen roses delivered before we got there. They were waiting on the table for her too.

Suzanne: From the very beginning we have been the most romantic couple you will ever find. That didn't change after I got diagnosed with MS. My husband is the most romantic man that God put on this earth. We love each other just as much today as we did when we first became a couple. Our intimacy is still just as wonderful. But sex is just one kind of intimacy. With Multiple Sclerosis you don't know what's going to happen tomorrow. You have to enjoy each day as well as each other.

Suzanne and Richard acknowledge the fact that it isn't always easy and they know that the road may get even more treacherous in the future. Like anyone facing the uncertainty that comes with the diagnosis of Multiple Sclerosis, they will continue to hope for the best. For now they consider themselves lucky and plan to enjoy every moment to the fullest.

Suzanne: I am one of the blessed ones. My family has been so supportive. The best lesson MS teaches you is to start living life like every day is your last one.

Jason DaSilva &
Alice Cook

❦

It is one thing to read about the harsh realities of
Multiple Sclerosis. It is another all together to actually
watch the very instant when this merciless disease attacks
a man's body. That shocking event was captured on
video and can be seen in Jason DaSilva's award-winning
documentary, *When I Walk*. The film, which was an

Official Selection of the 2013 Sundance Film Festival and won Best Canadian Feature at HotDoc 2013 follows Jason through his battle with Multiple Sclerosis.

The documentary opens in 2006. Jason is horsing around on the beach with his family. He's a handsome, athletic young man. The very picture of youthful vitality. He takes a seemingly harmless tumble in the sand. But from there the scene becomes heartbreaking to watch. He struggles mightily just to stand. Initially he laughs at his awkward efforts, but gradually both he and his family come to the realization that something is terribly wrong.

The audience becomes aware as well that they have just witnessed a young man at the very moment when his life has changed forever.

According to one of Jason's blog entries from those early days, "I wanted to capture this transformative experience—becoming disabled—in *When I Walk* because I hadn't seen it done before, and people need to see how a degenerative disease impacts the lives of those living with it. The first scene in the film is of me on the beach with my family. I brought my camera along to film the get-together, but the footage we captured meant more than I could have imagined. I fell down and couldn't get back up. It was the very first time my MS made something in my life go completely awry, made itself visible and impossible to ignore. What was supposed to be a nice family vacation turned into the inciting incident. Soon after, and encouraged by my family, I chose to not ignore my MS but to turn my camera on it instead. I had made films all my life, so making a film about the progression of the disease seemed a natural way for me to process the journey."

Jason DaSilva has Primary Progressive Multiple Sclerosis. And it is moving through his life like a freight train. That day on the beach, however, was not actually the beginning of Jason's journey with this terrible disease.

Jason: In 2004 I started feeling like I was walking off balance and I began to have blurry vision. During that first year of symptoms I didn't go to a doctor. I had no idea that what I was experiencing was MS. I think my mom mentioned that it could be MS, but I never really believe it. Unfortunately she was right. I was diagnosed in 2005.

Being unfamiliar with a diagnosis of Multiple Sclerosis causes many people to fear the worst, but Jason's lack of information allowed him to assume the opposite.

Jason: I thought that I would get over it, that it wouldn't be around forever. I believed that it would be gone at a certain point so I wasn't very worried. I just didn't think that there would be any problems going forward.

Jason's optimism would not prove to be well founded. His disease progression was rapid and devastating. In

2006, as he continued with his dream of making films, the disease began to morph and change in a way that would force him to alter nearly everything about his life.

Jason: It affected everything from being able to see the screen, to being able to use my hands. Even holding the camera was becoming more difficult. I lived life up until the age of twenty-five totally able-bodied and didn't have any challenges. I still think of myself like that every morning when I wake up. My psyche has not caught up with my reality.

But Jason was unwilling to give up on his art just because life was getting more difficult. He made changes to the way he did things, he adapted and continued on the path he had mapped out for himself in spite the obstacles that were before him. There was no way to know what would happen next, nobody to guide him through the daily trials.

He recorded those trials in his blog. "Also difficult was being forced to hand the camera over to my brother, my mother, my filmmaker friends, and my non-filmmaker friends. This was partly because of my MS (my vision was getting worse), but also because being in the shot meant that I couldn't capture it myself. This was perhaps the most frustrating part of making this film. I used to have total control over the camera and I was a meticulous shooter, so you can imagine the torture that was trying to give on-the-fly lessons in visual composition and camera exposure to my mother! The beautiful cinematography of my past was sacrificed, and my priority became capturing emotion. I found a new love for the expression of emotion, the subtlety of story, and capturing quietly compelling moments of human experience."

The film is not simply a tragic tale. It is also an inspiring love story, a tender account of a couple who learned that it is possible for love to flourish even under the most daunting circumstances. It reminds you of the joy and fulfillment that comes from finding that one person who really understands you and loves you wholeheartedly. Just at the moment where you can imagine a director calling for mood shift in the film, along comes Alice.

In 2009, Jason met the woman who would become the leading lady in his film and in his life. Alice Cook had decided to attend an MS support group in order to help her understand what her mother was experiencing. Jason happened to be attending the same meeting.

Alice: I was there because my Mom has the disease. She lives a long way away from me in another state. When her symptoms got really bad, I was having a hard time with the changes I was seeing in her from far away. I thought that learning more might help.

Jason: I started talking to Alice. She is a very pretty woman. I asked her if she wanted to go out after the meeting sometime and talk more. We met up for coffee.

Alice: It was very casual. In both of our minds, it was just coffee. He asked for my number but not like for a formal date.

That first informal outing led to a second date that was harder to play off as just casual. Alice could tell that there was something different about Jason, something that intrigued her. She was not sure about the idea of dating someone who had the same illness that caused her mother so much pain, however. So she went to the leading authority on the subject, her dad.

Alice: I had a long conversation with my dad. I asked him, "Can you date someone with MS?" He said "Yes, of course. I'm in love with your mother. Why would you let that get in the way?"

Although she couldn't help but draw parallels between her mother and Jason, the illness affected the two of them in very different ways.

Alice: When I met Jason he was using a walker and he had just gotten a scooter. My mom has Relapsing Remitting Multiple Sclerosis and she's still walking. She has a lot of cognitive challenges and fatigue, though.

Armed with her father's encouragement and her growing affection for this intriguing young man, Alice plunged forward into a romance.

Alice: In my past I might get a crush on a man or be a little curious about him, but as I got to know most of these other guys, I learned that they really weren't very remarkable after all. Jason was one of the most interesting people I had ever met. He had so much depth.

Jason quickly noticed that Alice different from his other friends too.

Jason: I think it was the openness that she had and the fact that I could talk about anything with her. I didn't feel strange talking about MS or the things I was experiencing. In New York people don't really talk about personal stuff.

The second date led to a third date, and Jason and Alice found themselves in falling in love. For the rest of their lives they will be able to look back at *When I Walk* and relive much of their courtship, including the time that Alice rented a scooter like Jason's so that she could see things from his perspective. One of the most endearing scenes in the movie is of them zooming around the Guggenheim Museum together. That willingness to put herself in his shoes set her apart and revealed her true character.

Jason: I think after that date I knew I was in love.

Jason's determination comes across in everything he does. He charges head-first into anything he sets his mind to. Getting Alice to be his one and only was no different.

Alice: He asked me to be his girlfriend. He was really cute. I don't remember exactly when, but he used the phrase "Will you be my girlfriend?" He was quite straightforward.

For Alice there wasn't a lot of adjustments that needed to be made or research that needed to be done. She was already familiar with the effects of Multiple Sclerosis. She had never known Jason prior to his diagnosis. This was the version of him that she fell in love with.

I think we are all at least a little afraid of our future. MS just makes us more aware that we don't know what that future is going to look like.

Alice: Any one of us could be diagnosed with something tomorrow. You don't know what the future holds for your partner or for you. Just because someone has MS doesn't make them less lovable.

Just six months into their dating life Jason made their commitment official with a proposal that was big on romance and sentiment, but maybe not so much on originality.

Alice: The official proposal was in Hawaii. We went to see Jason's dad and sister. We could still travel without anyone's help at that point and he could do many things for himself. We were going to dinner and somehow he got his dad to deliver the ring to the hotel.

When we went to the restaurant Jason had it with him. It was this beautiful, romantic restaurant on the water. Apparently it was also a pretty standard place to propose. Our waiter was really jaded because he had seen so many of them. He even said to us, "Yeah, whatever, everyone gets engaged here" and went on to explain that sometimes people came back later when they got divorced!

Shortly into their life together Alice realized that she also had a passion for film. Even if it wasn't the most lucrative career choice, it was important for both of them to pursue the dream together.

Alice: We're really focused on Jason's creative work. It's so engaging for us. We are doing what we love right now. We came together during uncertain times for both of us. Our financial picture is a patchwork of solutions, but we both work really hard. We're always working.

In the struggle to be helpful without being overbearing or overprotective, Alice leaves some of the heavy lifting to the caregivers who assist them.

Alice: I think it's difficult to know exactly how much you should or shouldn't do. He doesn't always ask for help when he needs it. I am very strategic in trying to allow other people to do transfers and carries. I know that we won't survive if I do everything for him.

One of the things that caught them by surprise was how isolating Multiple Sclerosis could be. They found that they weren't able to go to a lot of places simply because of accessibility issues. True to form, rather than allowing that to keep them at home, they decided to do something about it. They created an app that allows disabled people to learn how to navigate any city in America.

Alice: I think we would both agree that the disease is socially isolating. Sometimes that's the biggest challenge. It's the reason we developed AXSmap. We would make plans only to discover that the places we wanted to go weren't accessible.

Alice had another project in mind, as well. Even if the timing didn't seem perfect Alice really wanted to move into the next chapter of their life and start a family.

Alice: I was very upfront with Jason that having a family was really important to me. I was pretty determined and when I get like that it's hard to change my mind. I can be very stubborn about things. It was a leap of faith. I wasn't sure how I would be able to do this financially, but I was sure it would work out.

They named their son Jase. The joy and love that he brings to their life is priceless. You can sense their delight as they share how he loves trains and their pride when they talk about how much he is talking at the age of one and a half.

Jason: There are the challenges of not being able to do things that a normal father can do, but really it's been great. The next film is going to be about being a father with a disability. It's going to be called "Where You Go, I Go."

Alice: Life isn't fair for anyone. I don't see a lot of equality in life, so I guess I just sort of roll with it. On one hand I'm raising our child by myself. All of the physical challenges and care needs are my burden to bear. But the road Jason has to travel is a much more challenging one.

The strength and courage that Jason and Alice possess will most certainly be passed on to their son. The lessons they have learned from each other, they will also teach to him.

Alice: I can't believe how Jason just keeps going. He is such a resilient person who can't be stopped. He works harder than anyone I know. He has such tenacity. He's so committed. We are both committed to the social cause of helping others who are struggling and that bonds us together.

When facing one another at the altar most couples look into each other's eyes and see the promise of a beautiful future. Jason and Alice knew theirs would be one of many complexities and yet they forged ahead anyway believing that their love would guide the way.

And it did. It led them straight to a beautiful little boy with his father's sense of wonder and his mother's steady determination.

Bill & Pam Jackson

❧

Not every love story has a happy ending. But every now and then, even in the most heartbreaking of circumstances, you find a love so powerful, so genuine that even a painful conclusion doesn't in any way diminish the beauty of it.

Forty years ago it is doubtful that anyone would have cast Bill Jackson as the hero in a romantic saga. He was a down on his luck guy without a nickel in his pocket and certainly not recognizable as a potential suitor for a bright, attractive young lady who was trying to start a new chapter in her life.

Bill: I came to Duluth as a drunk in the early seventies. I was literally a homeless wino. I had been living on the street for a year, and had failed at rehab fourteen times. All I owned was a cardboard box with three pair of pants and two shirts to my name.

Pam Hultquist, a determined young woman of just twenty-three was working two jobs and trying to come to terms with the tragic death of her six-day old baby. The subsequent emotional toll of the painful loss brought about the end of her first marriage.

The last person in the world she needed to connect with was a man with more baggage than the lost and found department at JFK.

Bill: I noticed this beautiful girl working at J.C. Penny's and decided that I absolutely needed to meet her. I hounded her until she agreed to go out with me. Needless to say, no one else thought that was a good idea.

And yet for some unknown reason, Pam accepted Bill's offer of a cup of coffee and a friendly chat. Perhaps she had a fleeting moment of clairvoyance. How else could she have known that such a lowly vagabond would someday become her knight in shining armor? The two began to meet regularly just to talk. But long before he could be anyone's protector, Bill needed to save himself. Pam provided just the impetus he required to make the changes in his life that would allow someone like her to fall in love with him. It took Bill three weeks to work up the nerve just to kiss Pam goodnight, but he knew he was in love long before then.

Bill: Initially, I have to be honest, I'm a guy and she was a 5'7" beauty with auburn hair that went clear down to her waist. I was attracted to her looks. After sitting down and talking to her, I realized that she wasn't a flake or an airhead. Then I really knew I had to find a way to win her. She told me that if this was going to work, I was going to have to make some big changes, and so I did. That was the beginning of forty-two years of sobriety and my transformation into man we could both be proud of.

A year later, the cardboard box was long gone and he was finally ready to ask for her hand. But while he had smoothed over many of his rough edges, some still remained, as was evident in his less than romantic offer of marriage.

Bill: We were at Stoney Point, looking out over Lake Superior. At the time, it wasn't as nice as it is now. We were just sitting on this broken up wall and I looked at her and asked "How long are we gonna play this game, or are we gonna get 'er done?"

Miraculously, Pam wasn't put off by his prosaic proposal and said yes.

With just her parents looking on, in a dress she had made herself, Pam took a gigantic leap of faith and began a life with her reformed rogue.

Bill: I wasn't close to my family at that time and they didn't come up from down south for the wedding. They weren't nearly as optimistic about my conversion as Pam was. I didn't really blame them. After all, I had gotten married before and it didn't end well. I had owned a little bar in Florida. My ex-wife accused me of drinking all the profits, so I proved her right and took what we had left in the bank and just started driving. Two years later I was in Duluth, drunk and broke. I certainly wasn't the greatest person when I was drinking. It took my parents six years to talk to me again.

Everyone expected that alcohol would be the enemy the couple would battle. But unbeknownst to either of them, there was a more insurmountable foe waiting in the shadows. Bill had re-joined the army as a recruiter and was preparing to be sent off to fight in Desert Storm when the first troubling signs of what was to come emerged. Pam began experiencing tingling in her feet. Even though her doctors were not certain of the cause, Bill went to speak to his commanding officer about his concerns over her health. He was assured that if Pam became seriously ill, they would find a way to get him home. However, it wasn't the army that prevented Bill from being by Pam's side when the doctor delivered the heartbreaking fact that she had Primary Progressive

Multiple Sclerosis. Pam had decided to face that news alone.

Bill: She got her official diagnosis while I was deployed, but didn't tell me because she didn't want me to worry. When my unit arrived stateside, there was a huge gathering of family members waiting to welcome us home. I spotted Pam immediately in the crowd. I couldn't wait to get my arms around her. She must have decided that she wasn't going to ruin those first great moments together by telling me the truth. On the ride home she broke the news about her diagnosis. I was pretty ignorant about MS at the time and didn't really know what to expect.

Like any young couple, readjusting to life together after a military deployment was not without tribulations, but the challenges of Pam's declining health quickly took priority. Initially Pam's symptoms were fairly mild, but it wasn't long before walking became very difficult for her. Within just two short years she needed forearm crutches, and soon after was in a power chair.

Bill: When I came back, me and Pam were having some tough times, and it was …well, we were just having some tough times. But when I realized what she was up against, it changed things. Regardless of the fact that our marriage wasn't perfect, we said let's not worry about these problems, let's take care of this and we'll worry about the other shit on the way.

As her needs became greater, so did Bill's devotion. In the early stages of her disease, Pam was working at

University of Minnesota Duluth and determined to keep her job in spite of the challenges of Multiple Sclerosis. Every day Bill would help her out of bed in the morning, get her in her scooter, out to the truck, and help her into her office. At the end of every workday, he would be there waiting to help her come home. And during the day, if she ever had a problem, he would come running. But, regardless of Pam's resolve to keeping working, and Bill's unfailing assistance, it was a heartless supervisor that ultimately ended her career.

Bill: I don't like to use the word "hate" too much, but her supervisor was so evil that the word fits the way I felt about her. She did everything she could to force Pam out. The stress proved to be just too much for her. I think it really aggravated her symptoms.

It wasn't long before Pam lost what little mobility she had left. At the age of forty-eight, she became completely bedridden and would remain so for an unimaginable eleven years. Without hesitation, Bill quit his job and devoted his life to caring for his bride. For many recovering alcoholics, such an emotionally taxing situation might have caused a relapse, but Bill never even considered it.

Bill: How could I help her if I was drunk? There were times I would get frustrated thinking I wasn't doing enough. There were times when I hated everything about MS. But I was a combat medic in the army, so I knew I could take care of her. I never doubted that I would stay sober.

Tragically, over time Pam's spasticity became so severe that she could not even lie on her back anymore and was locked in a fetal position. She was to be confined to that position for seven long years, so rigid that it took two people to move her legs for a pillow to be put between them.

> *I did ask God on numerous occasions if He would just give this to me. I could handle it better than her. Give it to me, and let her be.*

Bill: I heard about a treatment that might help her. There were no guarantees and I had to fight like hell to get it approved, but if there was any chance that this medicine would relieve her pain, I wasn't going to stop until they gave it to her. Once she got it, things weren't as bad. I had a lot of guilt back then about being the healthy one. I still have some that I am carrying around. I'm not the most religious individual, even though my grandfather and uncle were ministers and I was a Sunday school teacher, but I did ask God on numerous occasions if He would just give this to me. I could handle it better than her. Give it to me, and let her be.

Of course there was no way for Bill to take Pam's illness away from her, but he did the next best thing. He became much more than just her spouse. He was her caregiver, her protector and her champion. Whatever Pam needed, whatever Pam wanted, he saw to it that she got it.

Bill: I made sure that the doctors and nurses gave her what she was supposed to have. I am a pretty easy-going guy, but if anyone gave Pam a hard time "nice" disappeared. I could take anything but someone being mean to her.

But fighting battles wasn't Bill's only way of showing his love for Pam. Bill also made sure that he brought a little joy into Pam's life whenever he could. He made every Friday night their date night by ordering a pizza and watching a movie with her in her bedroom. She once spotted a secretary's desk in a catalog that she thought was especially beautiful. Of course, Bill ordered it for her and patiently assembled it, even though he knew she'd never be able to sit at that desk.

However, it soon became apparent that even Bill's loving care was not enough. Pam's medical needs required that she be moved to a nursing home.

Bill: Even when she went into that home we still had our date nights. I would go there every day from eight in the morning to five at night and if she called me at three in the morning, I would go back. And I made sure that she had fresh flowers every day.

One Thanksgiving Bill even took a small rotisserie, a twelve pound turkey and all the fixings of a feast to Pam's room. He was determined to cook his wife a proper holiday meal.

Bill: The director said I couldn't do it. He said it wasn't allowed, but I told him "if you're gonna kick me out, you better bring some friends with you because you're not big enough!" She was not going to have processed turkey and cold beans for Thanksgiving if I had anything to say about it.

Doing sweet things for Pam seemed to come naturally for Bill. And his love for her grew in spite of the challenges they faced.

Bill: I think I was a decent husband, but she was an even better wife. She was one of the most caring people you'd ever meet. She was so supportive of me. Before she became sick Pam was always willing to help anyone. She had a heart as big as my living room and she would give you the clothes off her back. But she had some fire in her, too. You never mistook her generosity as a sign of weakness. I wouldn't say that Multiple Sclerosis caused our love to blossom, but it sure reinforced how much we loved each other. The vows say till death do you part, not until you become a pain in the ass. And I was a bigger pain in the ass than she ever was.

Caring for a spouse with a long term, degenerative disease is a challenge for even the most loving of partners. Patience is essential, tolerance a necessity.

Bill: You have to remember that it's gonna be a long ride. You can't get frustrated with each other. The person that is sick is frustrated because their mind is good, and the rest of their body doesn't cooperate. The person helping doesn't know if they are doing enough, or doing it right. If you don't really love your spouse, don't stick around. Let someone come in who does love her. Like many men, I was raised with the idea that you are supposed to take care of your woman. That was easy with Pam. I loved her so much.

If love was all it took, Pam would have walked out of the nursing home on the arm of her knight. But of course, that was not what happened. Primary Progressive Multiple Sclerosis was the dragon that Bill could not slay. In the fall of 2013, Pamela Jackson lost her battle with the disease. Her ashes were scattered across Lake Superior, not far from where Bill had proposed. Now he brings the flowers she always loved to the lake and places them gently in the water to watch them float away to her.

Bill: We knew as she got weaker, that the time was coming. I don't care how much time you've had to prepare though. If you are sitting next to the one you love and watch them take their last breath, there is no preparing for that. People say she's in a better place. That's bullshit. The better place is sitting next to me on the couch. I accept the fact that she is no longer in pain, and I'm glad that her pain is gone, but mine still goes on. The selfish part of me says I need her here. I bought this house for Pam. My plan was to bring her home. I knew if I got her in her chair, I could get her out on the deck. I promised her that she wasn't gonna die at a nursing home, that she was gonna be home, and I couldn't keep that promise. It has been a year now since her passing but I'm still having a tough time with that guilt. I am good at covering up my feelings with my jokes and my humor but talking about it all is kind of pushing that aside. I've got a part time job now that gets me out of the house once in a while. But when I come home at night, and I'm alone, it's hard. I have a large picture of Pam and me over the fireplace and everywhere I look around here, there are memories of Pam. She made so many of the things in this house. It gets a little tough. I just don't eat sometimes, and I love to eat. I don't sleep at night, I just kind of lay there and think and remember. Yes, it was hard at times, but the relationship was worth every bit of it. Would I do it again? Absolutely.

Bill would certainly not cast himself as the hero of this saga. He'd insist on awarding that title to Pam. But the truth is they both deserve the honor. Perhaps the most convincing proof of love's power is its ability to bring out the best in people. Bill and Pam proved to be one another's savior. And Pam is still playing her role. Even though the impetus to stay away from the bottle is no longer there, in Pam's memory, Bill Jackson remains a devoted and sober husband.

Tony & Kim Lokken

Their love story began on a beautiful summer day at the lake. She was an attractive, spirited girl and he, a shy country boy. She had forgotten her swimsuit, and was forced to substitute a friend's Wisconsin t-shirt and a pair of shorts to enjoy a dip in the cool water. Being from Wisconsin, the young man saw that as an opportunity to strike up a conversation. He teased her about being the only girl at the lake without a swimsuit and that opener eventually led to an exchange of phone numbers.

Kim: He was fun to talk to. He was also cute in that sweet and goofy way I've always liked.

Tony: Even in shorts and a t-shirt she was the prettiest girl at the lake. She seemed to have kind of an attitude that stuck in my mind. At that point I couldn't quite figure it out, but there was something that just stood out about her.

Obviously there was something about Tony that stood out in Kim's mind as well because a few days later she decided to call him. Unfortunately she had completely forgotten an important detail.

Kim: I just couldn't remember what he said his name was! I was hoping his voicemail would pick up so I could hear it. Thankfully it did and I avoided the embarrassment of having to admit that I had forgotten something so important. He called back and we talked a little and made plans to meet up.

But plans for a date didn't come together with ease. On the first attempt at a night out, the allure of a girls' night out won over the single mom.

Tony: Ha! She blew me off on the first date!

Kim: I had a four year old and didn't get out much. One of my friends called and said that she had a babysitter and asked if I wanted to go out. I cancelled my date with him to go out with my friend. I told him I didn't have a sitter. We ended up meeting up the next night and had cocktails together.

Although she cannot recall the specific moment that she found herself in love with Tony, throughout the course of the next three years they built a life together and made plans to be married.

Tony: (grinning) I grew on her.

Neither of them wanted a big wedding. They both felt that their love for one another was the most important consideration. So when the task of planning a formal affair became overwhelming to both of them, in a moment of spontaneity, they found someone on the internet who could legally perform a wedding. On a quiet moon-lit night they were married with a simple ceremony in the privacy of their living room. They decided to keep their clandestine nuptials a secret and went on with the scheduled wedding a month and a half later to satisfy their friends and family.

Together with Kim's daughter, Kennedy, they began their life as a married couple. About a year after they were married they found they were expecting a baby. But their idyllic life as a young family was about to change. In 2011, after they welcomed Boston, a baby brother for

Kennedy into their family, Kim began experiencing some strange symptoms.

Kim: Our son was five months old and I was nursing him. I would lift him to my shoulder to burp him and couldn't get my hand to move. I was also having dizzy spells. People thought it was just because I was nursing and tired from the demands of a newborn. They told me to drink more water. I went to my regular doctor and she told me that my symptoms were not due to any one cause. She told me I was probably suffering from carpal tunnel, as well as unexplained vertigo.

That seemed like a logical answer for the problems she was having. However, the variety and seriousness of these odd symptoms would continue to grow. Kim had previously been diagnosed with another auto-immune disease that can cause blood clots, and when she found herself not being able to speak correctly on multiple occasions she feared that she was having a stroke. When she called the doctor she was instructed to go to the Emergency Room immediately. At first she was reluctant to go but decided that the gravity of the situation warranted the trip. The couple discussed possible explanations for her issues during their hurried ride to the hospital. They both developed theories on what could be causing her problems, but the real answer would stun them both.

Kim: In the ER, they did an MRI as well as blood work. When we got the MRI results the doctor said that I didn't have a stroke but that I probably had Multiple Sclerosis.

Tony: We were both shocked. I remember seeing MS on the list of possible diagnosis for the symptoms she was having but I never believed that could really be what it was.

Kim: We always passed right by it because I thought I would know if I had that.

As is the case with many people unexpectedly diagnosed with an illness, the couple was left with more questions than answers and reeling from the news they had just received.

Tony: The doctor just left us sitting there, stunned and afraid. She simply told us to go see a neurologist. She didn't explain anything. All I could think was, what do we do now?

Kim: I didn't even know if you could die from it. The only person I knew that had it was my boss's wife. I knew she had a lot of trouble with it and I assumed I would end up in a wheelchair. That was my biggest fear I think. For a long time I would panic when I even saw someone in a wheelchair.

Tony: I didn't even know that much. A friend of mine had a sister that had it but I had never met her. I didn't know if this disease could actually take Kim away from me. That was my biggest fear by far.

The young couple now had to chart a course for how they would go on with their life, raise their children and deal with the uncertainties that the disease would present. They had barely begun their life together and now the future that they had dreamed of was under threat. Hope and possibility was replaced by fear and uncertainty. The vows that they had made just a couple of years earlier would be tested in ways that most couples never face.

Tony: I was so scared and I was really hoping that I was going to be able to handle everything. I was just thirty-two and didn't know anything about the disease or what might happen to Kim. I would tell Kim that I was nervous about it, but I never admitted how terrified I truly was. I was worried for the kids, too. I didn't know what would be in store for them.

Kim: Tony is typically a pretty emotional person, and I can tell when he has something on his mind. We are very open with communication but at that point we didn't really know what to say to each other. We were so busy with the kids. Trying to explain everything to our nine year old was overwhelming. I had so many questions that I wanted answers for. Would I still be able to work? And our son, Boston, was so young. I wondered what parts of his life I was going to miss out on. Would he understand and accept it?

While Boston was too young to understand the struggles that his mother faced, and will continue to face throughout his life, Kennedy has been very aware of the

114

severity of her mother's diagnosis from the beginning. But not surprisingly, she soon proved to her parents that she possessed the empathetic and compassionate personality of her mother.

Kim: Kenn is extremely intelligent. She was at the hospital with us on the day we found out what was wrong with me. We told her, "They think I may have MS. Together we'll learn what that means." When we contacted the MS society they sent us a little magazine and a DVD to help kids understand the disease. I think they really helped her a lot. She likes to know the specifics and those tools answered many of her questions. But at first it was a little hard for her because she didn't know what to expect. There are times when I have to tell her that I can't do things. However, she is always very understanding and comforting. It seems incredible sometimes that a child her age can be that sympathetic. When I worked up the courage to ask if she would be embarrassed if I was in a wheelchair she said "No, because you can still go places with me." What a kid!

Tony: Mainly I just hoped that Kim would still be able to go to Kennedy's games and choir concerts. So far she's been able to do all of that. I worry that she might not be able to do that for Boston, though. I guess that's been my main concern. Beyond the attendance at events, there's not much more I worry about as far as parenting is concerned. Kennedy and Kim have always been so close and Kim has been so open with her. Kennedy knows what her mom is going through. I couldn't have found a better wife to be a mother for my kids. She's like the ultimate mama bear. She will protect them at any cost.

Initially Kim's disease seemed to be progressing quickly. With each MRI the neurologist would find new lesions. It looked like they were facing the worst case scenario. Feeling as though they had no time to waste they decided on a course of treatment to hopefully slow the progression. Tony did everything he could to be helpful and supportive of his bride. He agreed to give her the injections that she would need to do three times a week even though it was incredibly difficult for him.

Tony: I had a hard time with it, keeping my hand still. I would get so nervous. Every time I did it I felt bad because I knew it would cause her pain.

Eventually Kim would take over, administering the medicine herself after Tony got the shots prepared for her. Though the medicine seemed to be effective in keeping the MS at bay it brought with it a whole new set of struggles for them to face together.

Kim: When I first started the medicine I got really sick with flu-like symptoms. My whole body ached. It was so bad. My hands and knees hurt all the time. I developed an ulcer and I started to lose a lot of hair. I noticed that as I lost it Tony would clean it up. He didn't want me to have to deal with it. One day I lost half my hair. It literally came out in a clump. Luckily he was there when it happened to help me with the shock of it all.

Having her husband beside her, as well as close friends who promised to go shopping for wigs with her, got Kim through the worst of the side effects. When her dosage was lowered, she began to tolerate the treatment much better. However, they would learn that keeping the disease from progressing didn't necessarily mean smooth sailing and symptom-free days. Like most people with Multiple Sclerosis, there is always evidence of its presence, even when the disease is not actively progressing.

Kim: The fatigue is probably my biggest hurdle. I finally found a medication that is sort of working. I get some hot sensations, or all of a sudden it will feel like I stepped on an ice cube. I also get some tingling and other strange sensations. Thankfully, my speech returned to normal. Sometimes I have some cognitive issues, figuring out a word, or what I am trying to say.

Desperate for some support, and knowing that there had to be other couples who were fighting battles similar to their own, Kim and Tony began to seek ways to connect with them. After a period of fruitless searching, they decided that if there was nowhere for them to turn, perhaps they should take it upon themselves to create the source of support and camaraderie they were looking for. They contacted the MS Society, and pitched the idea of a young couple's group. The suggestion was met with a great deal of enthusiasm. They just had to figure out how to make it a reality. Eventually, under Kim and

Tony's guidance, the group would take shape. It was to provide them, as well as the other couples, with the life preserver they so desperately needed in the sea of uncertainty that Multiple Sclerosis can cause.

Kim: We weren't really sure where we wanted to go with it. We knew that we wanted to form a group of couples who were at the same stage of life as we were. We began by meeting once a month just to talk. We try to go out to dinner now and then as well. One night we all went to comedy show together. But most of the time we simply choose a topic and allow everyone to share their experiences. The format might change from time to time but what's important is that we're talking.

Tony: We've had financial planning people come in to talk with us and we're even doing a yoga class for couples. We have based a lot of our meetings on Gary Chapman's book, The Five Love Languages. Kim and I found that book helpful for us, so we thought maybe it could help others too. Sometimes there are two or three couples, sometimes six or seven. We also do a lot on Facebook, so if some people can't make it to the meeting they can get caught up and interact with us there.

Although the common thread of life with Multiple Sclerosis ran throughout the assemblage of people, they had different reasons for walking through the doors. It was Tony and Kim's hope that regardless of what that motivation was each couple who participated in their group would leave feeling a little more hopeful. Being able to help others with the difficulties they faced, drawing on their empathy and getting others to do the same, helped the couple to look outside of their own issues. It gave them something to hold onto, something that made them feel like they were making a difference.

Kim: We had a couple who came in a while back who were really struggling. She was having a very difficult time with his diagnosis. When she came in she was really angry and she didn't seem to be able to see things from his point of view. He was feeling awful because he had to give up his career and couldn't work or drive. As facilitators, we asked the other people in the group how they would have dealt with these issues in order to help them to see each other's side.

Tony: This guy was ex-military. He used to ride motorcycles. I could see in his eyes how he now felt like less of a person. He was a pretty big guy. He used to be into weightlifting and strength training. You could tell that the weakness frustrated him and that he just wanted to be the strong person he used to be. I knew that he had a lot of pain. In the meetings she was very upfront about what she didn't like and I could tell that those words really hurt him. I think we all did a lot to help them gain some understanding of one another's fears though.

When any young couple recites the vows "...in sickness and in health", they are most likely imagining the majority of their lives being "in health", especially during the early years of their marriage. Although Tony and

Kim didn't have the benefit of a decade or more of experience, they soon learned the skills that are usually saved for the latter chapters of most people's marriage.

Tony: I hover. She calls me a kitty because you know how cats are always in your way? You turn around and there they are? I'm trying to be helpful but sometimes I just get in her way.

Kim: It is very hard for me to ask for help. I was alone with my daughter for years. Even prior to my diagnosis I wasn't good at asking for help. Trying to accept my limitations and what I can and can't do is frustrating. Sometimes I do too much and I pay for it. My mom comes over and wants to do the dishes and I used to tell her not to, but I finally started accepting her help. I appreciate the fact that I have a mom who wants to do the dishes for me.

Throughout the life of every married couple romance ebbs and flows with the tide that is daily life. But Kim and Tony had two of the biggest hurdles imaginable to leap over all at once - a toddler and a chronic illness. But with the same attitude of openness and acceptance that they approach the young couples' group they established they find ways to make time for each other and keep their love strong.

Kim: When we're not being very romantic it's hard to know if it's the MS or just life in general, especially life with a three year old. I think sometimes things slow down even though you may not want them to. There never seems to be enough time. I'm tired and he's been up since 4am.

Tony: I do feel bad sometimes because I know she's tired and she's been dealing with our son all day. I'd like to wake her up in the morning when we could have some time to ourselves but I like her to sleep when she has a chance to.

Kim: I think part of it is just not feeling very attractive too. When I am tired and not feeling good about myself I'm thinking he probably doesn't want me anyway.

Tony: And I feel bad for wanting her when she's not feeling good.

Kim: So we find ways to let one another know that we are thinking about each other. We have these little books that we use to write notes to each other and then we leave them somewhere to be found. Sometimes it's just a quick "I love you" but at least he knows I was thinking about him. We also have what we call our "closet dates". If we can't find a sitter or don't have time to go out, I will grab a snack and we go hide in the closet to enjoy a quick bite and chat. The kids don't know where we are. Even if it's just for five minutes we get some time to ourselves!

Many people who live with this disease will tell you that plans become a thing of the past. Whether it's plans with friends for the weekend or the overall plan for how your life is going to go - there is just no way of knowing what tomorrow will bring. That inability to make or to keep plans causes some people to avoid going out with friends at all. Trying to find a balance between taking care of yourself and becoming socially withdrawn is yet another strategic dance that needs to be practiced by couples facing illness. Having a partner who you can literally as well as metaphorically lean on is imperative. Venturing out on your own can sometimes seem overwhelming.

Tony: I try to push her to do things with her friends sometimes too. I think it's important for us to do things separately as well together.

Kim: I think I tend to become a hermit sometimes. If I feel really tired I don't want to get ready and go out. Sometimes it's not even that I feel like I am going to have an issue, but what if I do and nobody understands? I think sometimes I lean a lot on him. If he's going with me somewhere I just feel better. I have been trying to push myself not to do that because I like to go do things on my own. But still I fear that I'm not going to be okay or that people aren't going to understand. What if my hands or legs are shaking and I just want to go home?

Gauging other people's reactions and levels of understanding is something that those with a disability do on a daily basis. They may feel concerned that their symptoms will make people uneasy or unsure of what to say. There are the coddlers to deal with, those who somehow manage to maintain a look of pity throughout entire conversations. Then there are the "ignorance is bliss" individuals who avoid any mention of the illness.

Kim: I am kind of disappointed by my parents' reaction. I think that some of it might be their age. I feel like they didn't really learn a lot about MS after I was diagnosed. I think it's hard for them to grasp what's going on. I mentioned it several times, asking them to just read about it. I wish that they understood a little bit more. They help me a lot and I'm grateful for that, but sometimes you want to talk to your mother about what's going on and you want her to understand.

When people are asked what they would do if they knew they only had a week left to live, the array of answers given is infinite. The answer most often given, though, is that they would try to fit in those experiences that they always assumed they would have more time to complete. One of the positive effects of being diagnosed with a degenerative disease is that it creates an urgency to do things that you aren't certain you will be able to do much longer. Kim and Tony decided to seize the time when her health and abilities still enabled her to travel. The two splurged on a few unforgettable adventures. They created lifelong memories during a trip to Ireland and enjoyed Kim's dream vacation in Greece.

But appreciating time together has not been their only gift to one another. The truths they learned as they weathered this crisis are priceless. They have given the couple an indication of each other's real character. These insights are rarely accessed in the course of everyday existence.

Kim: There is a lot that I have learned about Tony since I got sick. I would have never guessed that he would have been as good as he is with everything. I think he's really stepped up to the plate a lot more than I thought he could. Not that I didn't think he would, but it's above and beyond. He is way more understanding and accepting than I could have ever hoped for. He is very considerate. I don't even have to ask for his help.

> *I would tell a man whose wife was diagnosed with this disease that she's still the woman you know and love. Be patient with her.*

Tony: I am amazed by how strong her drive is to really make things better for people in general. I knew that she was like this before her diagnosis but man she really goes out of her way to make so many other people just feel better about themselves or their situation. She has a gift. We knew someone who found out they had Parkinson's. Kim baked her a bunch of treats and cooked some dinners that she could freeze. The two of them even enjoyed a picnic one day. She is the most helpful and considerate woman I have ever known.

Sometimes people also learn a lot about themselves in a time of trials.

Tony: I didn't grow up around anyone who was sick. I feel like Kim's disease has taught me a lot about patience. That trait is one of the things I have gained as well as the ability to empathize with people. I have met so many people who have MS and it's taught me a lot more about compassion for others. I feel like the things that I have learned the last few years have been really humbling. I wish I would have understood all of this before Kim's diagnosis but I didn't know any other way of being back then.

Being left in that hospital room to try and process the life altering news they had just received is a memory that will forever haunt the young couple. They would have benefitted tremendously from the wisdom of others who had gone through that moment before them. That is exactly why the two of them formed the young couples' support group.

Kim: If I was able to speak to a couple who had just received that news, I think the most important thing I would want them to know is that life isn't over. This doesn't mean that you are heading down any certain path. You can still pick your path. At the beginning I felt like my future was now chosen for me. I think it is so important to know that you aren't alone, too. So many people are struggling with the exact same issues. Someone once asked us what we get out of our couples group. I told them that we still need that support too. We need it so that we can make it through the hard days. It is essential as well to try to understand what your partner is experiencing. I really strive to put myself in Tony's shoes. I can't forget that he needs things too. Even if it's just a small gesture, I will just send him an email telling him I appreciate him. Sometimes it is the little things, the ones that just take a couple minutes that are the key to keeping our relationship strong.

Tony: Things are going to happen but if you can work through it with your partner you will come out far stronger than you were before.

When someone is diagnosed with a disease like MS they are faced with a barrage of choices...how to treat it, what doctor to see. You have to decide who you will tell and how you will break the news. As things progress you may have to choose when to start using an assistive device. You have to decide when to go to the hospital and when it's best to just ride out the pain. Sometimes just making the choice to get out of bed can be emotionally and physically painful. In the face of so many arduous decisions there was a very uncomplicated and undeniable one that Kim and Tony made in their apartment on that moonlit night.

They chose each other. They chose love.

photo by Sandra Cifo

Marty & Dave Rice

❧

He catches a glimpse of a smiling, blonde off-duty flight attendant from across an airport terminal and is stunned by her beauty. He tries to charm her into sitting next to him on the plane. She acts coy, but unbeknownst to him covertly secures her seat by him at the flight desk. After a lively conversation and a lot of flirting, a tongue-in-cheek marriage proposal is offered and scribbled on an air sickness bag that would someday end up framed and hung next to their wedding photo. It sounds like a movie script, but for Marty and David Rice, it's their real life love story. But like so many cinematic romances, mixed in with the passion there would also be pain.

Mary: He was so sweet and we were flirting like crazy. Halfway through the flight, I asked him to marry me, and he said yes. I told him to write it down so it would be legal.

Dave: Sure I was attracted to her, but it was her personality that I fell in love with on that plane. She was upbeat and positive and sweet. She was smart and witty. All of those things really appealed to me.

But before Dave could make good on his promise, he had to secure a first date.

Dave: Even though I was on my way to San Francisco, I asked her if I got off in Billings, would she go out with me that night.

Marty: I said no, and then David asked where I was staying so he could at least call me. But in the scramble of disembarking, I didn't have a chance to tell him the name of my hotel. That night the phone rang, and it was him. I asked "How did you find me?"

Dave: I called the information operator, and asked "What is the name of the biggest hotel in Billings, Montana?" I called the desk clerk for that hotel and asked to be connected to Martha Peterson's room. It was really pretty easy. Back in those days people were more accommodating. Besides, I knew I loved her already and I wasn't about to let her slip away.

And so began a long distance love affair. David was working in the Chancellor's office at UC Berkley in San Francisco, and Marty was based out of Minneapolis. One year later Marty moved to the area and David fulfilled his promise. The two were married and became proof that love at first sight not only exists but can actually lead to years of joy and devotion.

Two and a half years later they welcomed their daughter, Jenny. Her birth was followed in two years by the birth of a son, James, who the family called Jamie. Their home was filled with laughter, chaos and most of all, love.

But there was a shadow over the couple's happiness that was becoming increasingly difficult to ignore.

Marty: When my son was three years old I started to feel tingling in my toes. I told David what was happening. Then the fatigue started setting in. He was so sweet. He said if your body is telling you to rest, just rest. This was 1982 and I was thirty years old.

Choosing to do her own research, she scoured medical books in the library about her increasingly troubling symptoms, and began to fear that all the signs were pointing towards to Multiple Sclerosis. But she kept her suspicions from everyone but her husband, even going so far as to hide the medical books from her children. It would be eleven long years before she confirmed her self-diagnosis with a doctor.

She had both emotional and financial reasons for waiting that long.

Marty: I hid everything up until 1993. My mother was such a dear, sweet woman, and there was never a daughter who was loved more than I was. I knew this would break her heart and I just couldn't tell her. Dave was the only one I confided in. After all, he is my best friend. He knew everything from the very beginning.

David had just started his own consulting firm and Marty also feared that a pre-existing condition would drive up the cost of their health insurance, and besides, she had read that there was no cure for this disease.

Marty: In some ways, a little bit of knowledge is a dangerous thing. I didn't realize that a few of the symptoms could have been handled with medication and that I had been struggling needlessly.

In 1993, she read an article about a new treatment that had just been approved for MS and decided that it was finally time to see if there was some means of addressing her worsening problems. She now needed to constantly brace herself using the walls of their home as she walked. When she did finally make an appointment, however, the first doctor she saw dismissed her concerns.

Marty: He said I was simply a stressed out mom and I knew that was crap. It was devastating to have my problem trivialized like that.

David: I felt that he was sort of an arrogant guy. He said that she should just go home, that she was a hard working mother and probably had too much salt in her diet. I urged her to get a second opinion.

Marty: I went to a female doctor and - bless her heart - she was so good to me. I sat in her office and cried and told her everything that had been happening to me. She immediately sent me for an MRI. I was right. It was Multiple Sclerosis. When we got home, we talked with our children. We told them what I had and that I had known something was wrong for quite a while, but now we had a name for it. I assured them that I wasn't to going to die from it and that things really weren't going to change. If they had any questions, they could ask me and if I didn't know the answer I would find it. I told them that it wasn't a secret anymore. They could tell people if they wanted to. My son, being twelve and playing every sport in the world, was concerned that I was going to be in a wheelchair. I told him that I didn't know, but if I was, that would be alright, too.

Although the news was startling to their children, both Marty and Dave had long been bracing themselves for the diagnosis.

Dave: It didn't rattle me because Marty had done so much research and I expected it. I am a realist and I know life can be pretty random. Some people can pitch a baseball and some people can't;

some people get a disease, and some don't. We all get dealt different kinds of hands, and this was hers. For me, it was most important that I was supportive of her.

Even though she had suspected MS, hearing the words made the reality of what was ahead difficult to accept. Marty began to worry not only about her own future, but that of her family as well.

Marty: How am I going to take care of my family? I did a lot of work with my hands and loved to cook. I was a Girl Scout and a Cub Scout leader, as well as a parent advisor. I had a therapy dog that I would bring to the hospital to visit with people who were ill and would never recover. I could not have imagined myself in that hospital.

After a short period of worry however, her optimistic spirit came through and she was ready for whatever was ahead of her.

Marty: Long ago I made peace with this. If this is the hand I was dealt I am going to play it to the best of my ability.

There were changes that would need to be made and that meant different sacrifices and adjustments for each of them, but everyone in the family was willing to do whatever was necessary.

Dave: I began adjusting my schedule to allow more time. For instance if James was playing baseball and we had to walk a long way on uneven ground it would take us longer. It was really a

132

matter of me trying to adjust my thinking to always add time and take extra things into consideration like making sure that Marty wasn't directly in the sun. We learned to always carry an umbrella. There is also an issue of protection. When you are in a crowd of people, particularly high school kids, I would keep her close to avoid collisions. We have always been pretty openly affectionate and we are usually holding each other's hand anyway.

Arm in arm they would arrive at different events and then wait until the crowd left to make their exit. Dave also took a job closer to home so that he could be there if Marty needed him.

> *Our bodies are just our packaging. The essence of who you are doesn't change.*

Marty: We have always been a team. Multiple Sclerosis just caused us to become more organized and to work together even better.

Looking to recruit some more support players for their team they decided to attend a group for people with MS and their families. It didn't turn out to be what they needed.

Marty: We went to this support group and I think I must have been born on a sunny day because I couldn't understand why all these people were so damned depressed. I felt like I couldn't keep going to it. On the other hand, there was a woman at the school who had just been diagnosed and she reached out to me. I found my own group of people for support and friendship. Anybody who lives long enough is bound to get something. As you age you might get gray hair, you might get bigger, you might get smaller. Even when MS took away my ability to play the piano or something like that I was still the same person. The essence of who you are doesn't change.

As her mobility issues increased and walking became more difficult for Marty, she was faced with what is a harsh reality for many people with MS. It was time to transition into the next phase of assistive equipment.

Marty: It was 2004 when I went into a wheelchair. I was only 52 years old. And at that time I was falling a lot. I mean I had sprained ankles like you wouldn't believe because I was falling all the time. The transition was bittersweet. It had taken so much energy to do anything. When I was in the chair I didn't have to use all my energy just to get someplace. We made some adjustments to our home. Luckily we live in a ranch style home so it wasn't difficult. We widened the bedroom door and remodeled the bathroom. We put in a shower so that they can just wheel me right in there.

As her dependence on others gradually increased, it was important to both of them that she not lose the spunk and zest for life that she had always possessed.

Dave: Marty has the perfect personality for this. She's like the head cheerleader in school. She has a desire to keep other people upbeat. She has a really strong will. She has always tried to do everything and to this day she is still the same way. She will do as much as she can on her own. Before she got the wheelchair she would often fall. My son or I would pick her up. It was difficult because Marty never wanted to impose on anyone, but it became difficult for her to stay safe. It was important that we were around as much as we could be without taking away her initiative to take care of herself or do things on her own. Sometimes I am afraid I am a little over protective and she doesn't like that.

Marty: I think he can be very overprotective. I love him for it but sometimes it just drives me crazy. He is a caretaker by nature, and I love that, but sometimes it can be a bit much. When I was in the hospital they called me the "I'd rather do it myself" lady. If there is something I can do myself I would much prefer that.

Children who are raised in a home where one of their parents has a disability are exposed to an entirely different set of circumstances and realities than children with healthy parents. Often parents worry about the things that their children will miss out on or the things that they are unable to help them with, but in truth the experience can have more positive influence on them then negative.

Marty: I can tell you one thing for sure. My MS has made my children a lot more compassionate. If they see somebody in the store or on the street and they look like they need help, my son and daughter won't hesitate to provide it.

135

Marty and Dave's daughter, Jennifer, has actually gone on to make a career out of helping people with Multiple Sclerosis. In her role as Donor Relations Coordinator, Jennifer works with supporters of the NMSS to help raise awareness and encourage funding for MS research, programs and services for people affected by the disease.

Jennifer: Because I've lived with my mother's diagnosis for almost thirty years I take my job personally. I'm very driven as result. For so many years I felt hopeless. But I feel such a sense of empowerment with the work I do now. I started out as a volunteer, doing whatever they needed in the office and participating in walks because it made me feel like I was doing something to further the mission. When they offered me a position I had no problem leaving my career in marketing and advertising. This work touches my soul. It means so much more to me than anything I've ever done. When I talk with people who have been affected by the disease and I tell them that my mom has MS they realize that I understand, that I can empathize. I grow and gain so much when I connect with people too. I sincerely get much more than I give. This job has been a tremendous blessing for me.

Dave: I think Marty hit it on the head. It's made them much more compassionate and caring. I think the only negative is the frustration they feel. They wish their mother didn't have this disease. They would like to be able to do things for and with her that are impossible. They aren't mad at her. They are mad at what the disease has taken from her and how it has limited their relationship with her.

Both Jennifer and Jamie have been distressed by the toll MS has had on their mother. But the compassion and concern they learned has clearly been a driving force in their life. But it wasn't just their mother's challenges that shaped their personalities. From a young age Marty and Dave's kids played a role in helping others too.

Dave: I coached little league for years. There is a group called the Challenger Division. That's where children with challenges are teamed up with the regular players from the other teams. Each child is paired up with a buddy. The teams play against each other, and the rules are that you have to have a barbeque after the game, every child has to play and every game ends in a tie. It's great for the little leaguers because they form strong bonds with those kids. Jamie was a buddy and he loved that role.

Marty: When Jamie was a teenager and it came out that medical marijuana was approved for MS he thought that was the coolest thing in the world. I was like a hero! And I went on a bar crawl with my daughter when she turned thirty. People hopped on the back of my chair when they'd had a bit too much to drink. In San Francisco my chair goes up the hills like a dream!

Dave: Now our granddaughter crawls all over her scooter. Instead of pony rides she has granny rides!

Even couples who find a way to live with the adjustments that disability requires have to accept the inevitable truth is that Multiple Sclerosis changes the complexities of your relationship as a couple. The trick is to find the silver lining at those times, something that Marty and Dave seem to be experts at.

Marty: I guess as far as intimacy goes...that changed a little bit but as far as affection, I still can't keep my hands off of him!

David: Things changed in that respect. Before MS we might have gone to Carmel for a weekend but when you have to take so much with you, you don't get out as much as you did when you were able bodied. Instead of taking a long trip somewhere we will spend the night in San Francisco. Over many years things changed but the loving connection isn't broken, it's just different.

Marty: He does incredibly personal stuff for me and yet he still kisses me like he really loves me; kissing that person that I am, and forgetting about having to take care of the package that I'm in.

They have also found that keeping a sense of humor is crucial.

Marty: I said to him the other day, "You know, you really meant that for better or for worse, for sickness and health stuff." He looked at me and said, "Yeah, just like you meant that obey part!"

Outside of their family circle some of the reactions to her illness weren't as favorable. They have found that some people backed away, especially as the illness progressed. The couple found it to be an interesting study in human nature and definitely a test of who their true friends were...the ones that meant it when they said they would stick by them.

Marty: When everybody found out that I had MS they stopped asking me to volunteer. Friends calling and inviting us to do things or just stopping by...a lot of that ended too. I think people thought they were going to bother us or they didn't want to interrupt me. I don't know if they were afraid of offending me. I was surprised by the way some people handled it. Even some of the kid's friends started acting differently. We had an open door policy but that slowed down because I think people don't want to impose. Most people don't know what to say. I just told them that my door is wide open and then some people started coming back around. We would invite people in, the ones that picked up on it were the ones that have stayed our close friends. And others who were afraid kind of faded away. At our home our friends don't knock, they just come in.

Some people seem to just be built for crisis. They handle difficult situations with grace and courage and appear undaunted by the curveballs that life throws at them. The precariousness of the situation is not lost on them but they gather their wits about them and do what they need to with a smile on their face. Witnessing someone you love struggle is difficult. Marty considers herself the luckiest woman in the world to have David by her side as she goes through her journey with MS. And David is continually amazed by Marty's eternal optimism and strength.

Marty: Sprinkled in with the MS I also had spinal fusion. Four years ago I fell out of my shower chair and needed stitches in my

139

face. I was home with a broken femur for a week without knowing it. It was a very difficult time when I had to be on Chemo. Then I had a bladder infection that put me in the hospital for a month. But Dave is just a champ. There are only two things that scare me - anything happening to David or my children. I live with MS. I stare it in the face every day. What else do I have to be afraid of?

Rather than focusing on the tragedy and loss of their situation the family chooses to see the more favorable things that Multiple Sclerosis has instilled in all of them, as well as the people around them.

David: Our family is stronger than most and sort of under an umbrella of compassion. It's created a very strong bond between us. I think our friends and neighbors recognize our family as being a pretty solid unit. And MS, while it has been a negative in many ways, it created that positive energy that other families take note of. We are very resilient. Not only did MS strengthen the four of us but it made us a noteworthy family in the community. People imagine the weight of the challenges as being negative, but see us overcoming them.

Marty: We really don't sweat the small stuff. The truth is, I can't think of anybody in the world I would trade places with.

The words that David would choose to share with a couple that has recently received the same diagnosis as his beloved wife speak volumes as to why their love has remained so strong throughout their journey of the past three decades.

David: I would say that it's incredibly important to keep a sense of humor and to be positive. No matter what happens, if you can kind of laugh at things, the ridiculousness of it, it keeps you in a positive spirit. You have to be strong. There is no room with this disease to be weak. You have to find a way to be strong and if you prepare yourself for that you will be successful. If you throw yourself a pity party you're going to end up failing in the relationship. Look at the core of the person you are with, don't look at the disability. Remember what it is that makes that person special and focus on that. Things can change but the core stays the same.

Marty has a special message taped to her refrigerator door, one that she looks at every day. It has been her inspiration and at times, the source of her courage.

"Sometimes it may seem like a battle to rise above the feelings of grief or overwhelming anger that periodically occur. Although those feelings are real, they need not be permanent or on-going. Acknowledge your emotions then look to find a glimmer of hope. Hope is there in the things that MS doesn't take from you, such as the ability to love, share and communicate. One thing you will always keep is the ability to choose your attitude. Knowing this will empower you to become stronger than MS."

Insert any challenge in the place of "MS" and the message becomes one that perhaps we should all read every day. And while the words may be Marty's guiding force, it is the love and devotion of her family that allows her to absorb and embody their significance.

photo by Steve Jessmore

Dan & Jennifer Digmann

❧

Most people search for buried treasure on sunken ships or in secret pirate caves. But when Jennifer Digmann decided to try her luck at an MS seminar in an elementary school gym, most people would have considered that a long shot at best. Who would imagine that riches could be hidden in such an unlikely spot? What kind of strange map would lead a treasure hunter to explore such an unlikely location? It would surely take a miracle to find anything of value there.

143

But a miracle was just what Jennifer needed. Up until this point it seemed that not many had come her way.

It was 2002 and she had every reason to be skeptical that a fantasy, happy-ever-after ending was in the cards for her. At twenty-eight years of age she had already seen so many of her dreams slip from her hands.

Five years earlier she had been well on her way in life. She was just six months out of college and had landed her first real job. As a bright, beautiful and talented young woman it seemed as though there was no limit to what she could achieve. A successful career, an active social life...maybe even a husband and a family...all seemed to be in her future.

Then the unthinkable happened.

The day began in a totally unremarkable fashion. Jennifer had gone to work, chatted with friends, made plans for the weekend. But through it all she kept noticing something odd. Her vision was not quite right. In fact it was becoming very wrong as the day wore on. One eye refused to move and she was seeing double of everything. Her friends urged her to see a doctor right away.

Jennifer: The doctor I saw felt that I should see an ophthalmologist. Then the ophthalmologist sent me to a neurologist. It didn't take him long to diagnosis me with Multiple Sclerosis. The whole nightmare happened in a mere forty-eight hours. I was shocked and there were a lot of tears shed. I was extremely sad and very afraid that I would never walk again.

It took five years for Jennifer's fears to be realized. Before she even reached thirty, before her career could get started, before her life could really begin she was in a wheelchair. The progression of her disease was steady but Jennifer still held out hope that it could be reversed.

Jennifer: Every summer the disease would flare up a little. The first summer I saw a physical therapist, then I needed a cane, then a large based cane, and then a walker. Within five years I started to fall quite often. I fell in the shower one day. I couldn't make my legs work. I was just so clumsy. It was time for a wheelchair but I didn't think that I would be in it for very long. The first day I had it I thought this was just going to be until I got a little stronger. But that was not the case. Thank goodness I had the people at the MS Society to turn to. My chapter of the National MS Society had prepared me for many things and connected me with others who were facing the challenges of this disease. From these connections I developed lifelong friends. When I was first diagnosed I had some doubts about my ability to handle what was happening, but I never once doubted my support system.

Connecting with her local chapter of the National MS Society had been a vital key to her adjustment process. But even the caring people of her chapter were not able to provide that magical happy ending that she was still hoping for. When they announced that a seminar was being offered for women who had had to put their dreams on hold, called "Finding Your Buried Treasure" Jennifer decided that maybe it would provide a route to the life she sought. Little did she know that her map to happiness would lead her to a young man named Dan.

Jennifer: I was expecting this program to be women only, so when a man walked in, especially a very cute man, I wondered whose boyfriend or husband he was.

Dan: Someone forgot to write on the announcement that the program was supposed to be for women! In fact the program manager for the MS society called and invited me to come down to the event. It was about an hour and a half from my home but it was a Saturday and I had nothing else I intended to do. When I arrived the program manager met me at the registration and suggested that I sit at Jennifer's table.

Clearly there was some matchmaking at work even though both of them were unaware of it.

Jennifer: Dan has the friendliest smile. He was really focused and added a lot to the conversation. I was the table leader and I could always look to Dan to contribute something...and he is awfully cute. Did I mention that?

The program manager had obviously been correct in her assumption that these two would be attracted to one another.

Dan: She thought that because we were both young and had MS, we might have a lot to talk about. When I first arrived, I kept wondering who is this Jennifer person she was talking about because she wasn't at the table. When she pulled up in her wheelchair I was thinking I had to bring my "A" game that day because I thought she was cute too. When the conference was over I hung around because I didn't want this to be the last time I saw her. I helped clean the place up while I was waiting for her to be alone. Finally she stopped talking to other people and I asked her for her email. The next day I went into work and told my friend "I met the woman I am going to be married to and you're going to be my best man."

Dan's first step was to compose the perfect email stating his desire to get to know her better. It was a task that proved to be more challenging than he expected.

Dan: I sat at my computer for three hours writing a two paragraph email to her. I really wanted to find just the right words. I wanted to express my feelings but I didn't want to sound like a stalker! I think I kind of left it open ended as far as getting together.

The wording was perfect but unfortunately a formal date would be sidelined by Jennifer's illness and a hospitalization. Such an unsettling development might have put a damper on a typical budding relationship. But not theirs.

Jennifer: Just a few weeks after we met I had to go into the hospital for a treatment. Dan drove nearly two hours to come and visit me.

It was Thanksgiving and he brought me pecan pie. He sat on the edge of my hospital bed and...this is the best part...he fed it to me! He was so sweet and so endearing. Especially considering that I had been in the hospital for four days and I looked like hell. I had an IV in my arm and was wearing a hospital gown and he treats me like I am the most beautiful woman on earth! We had only been talking on the phone up to this point. We hadn't even gone on our first date yet. I said to myself, "oh my gosh, this man is fantastic!"

While their first date wasn't quite the romantic adventure they might have envisioned, it was an experience that solidified in Jennifer's mind that this man was exactly the "buried treasure" she was hoping to find.

Jennifer: We weren't even alone on our first date. My grandfather was a baseball player at the University of Michigan and he was being inducted into the Sports Hall of Fame. I asked Dan if he would like to go to the ceremony with me...and my entire family!

Dan: I truly felt at home with them right away.

Jennifer: Everyone loved him. From that day on he became part of my family.

Three years later Dan officially became a member of the clan by marrying Jennifer. The two shared so much in common. They both love music, fantasy football and socializing with friends.

Unfortunately they also share an incurable disease.

Dan: In 1999 I was experiencing a strange numbness in my chest and some odd tingling sensations. That's when they started to run tests. After getting a spinal tap, I was formally diagnosed with Multiple Sclerosis on Valentine's Day of 2000. I actually suspected it and the formal diagnosis was somewhat of a relief. When you get a formal diagnosis and you know what you are dealing with you can start treating it. I think you always fear the worst. It is really the fear of the unknown. But I have a good foundation of faith, family and friends. I knew I could handle it, I just didn't know what I was going to have to handle. I had just started my job at the university. Here it was only a month and a half later and I'm diagnosed with this disease. Fortunately I was still able to continue my work. I can't feel my fingers anymore so I'm not exactly a great typist, but I get by and I've even had two promotions.

Every newly married couple has adjustments to make. For Dan and Jennifer the accommodations often revolved around understanding each other's limitations and strengths.

Jennifer: Dan has never known me to walk. I have been in a wheelchair since we met. When I first went into a wheelchair I thought I was never going to meet anyone. No one would want to date me. But then I meet this incredible man. My disease has progressed over the years but we change and we grow together. He was more overprotective when we first got married but because we have changed together, we've worked it out.

As with many couples who live with a chronic illness learning how to, and more importantly, when to step in with assistance or ask for help was sometimes a challenge for Dan and Jennifer.

Dan: I think a lot of that came with time and communication. Your tendency as a man is to want to step in and do things for her. But a lot of times what she needs is just for me to be empathetic. I don't want her to feel that she can't do as much as she used to but at the same time she has to recognize when she needs to ask for the help.

Jennifer: If it's something I know I can't do, that's easy. But if it's something I want to be able to do for myself or something that I think I should be able to do and I'm forced to ask for help, I can get a little crabby about it.

It is clear that Jennifer's disease progression has been much more dramatic than Dan's. The disparity between their limitations and challenges can sometimes cause each of them to feel a little concerned about the future and how they will handle the changes ahead.

Jennifer: To say that we've handled the difference between our challenges would be a lie. The issue still does come up from time to time. I think it's not fair to Dan and he shouldn't have to deal with all of my problems and needs. But through constant communication and reminding myself that he doesn't do this because he's obligated. He does it because he loves me. I'm getting better about accepting his help. And I don't support him because I have to, I do it because I want to.

Dan: I fear that my disease could progress too. Mostly I fear that because it would be so unfair to her. I went for a walk on the day I met Jennifer. I realized that I had just met a girl who might need me to stay healthy. Later on I started running again too. I wasn't winning races but I was holding my own. Did I feel guilty running when my wife was sitting home and couldn't walk? No. When you are on an airplane they tell you to put your own mask on first, then one on your child because you need to be able to take care of him. I am blessed that I haven't developed a worse case of MS so that I can be here for her.

> *I think it's vital to focus on how much I love him, not what I can or cannot do.*

Maybe another woman would be resentful of the freedom that her husband's relatively mild illness afforded him. But not Jennifer.

Jennifer: I would be angry with Dan if he wasn't doing every single thing he can. I can't walk anymore and I want him to walk for me. I am so proud when I see him at the finish line. I really feel like he's doing it for both of us.

Traditionally the cheering spouse is there at the race's end to offer a big hug and a kiss of congratulations. But even that small gesture of affection is something that

151

Dan and Jennifer have had to forgo. A symptom of her MS causes painful, electric sensations if she tries to form her lips into a kiss.

Jennifer: Dan is happy to kiss me on my forehead or hug me or sit next to me on the couch and hold my hand. Intimacy in our relationship is so much more than the carnal act. Those moments, the tender moments where he's holding my hand, that's what is important. His hands get really tired and when I want to do something nice for him I'll rub them.

Dan: The reality is that I love her even more than I did when we first got married. I love bringing her dinner over to her or doing some small favor. I know that she feels guilty sometimes but I always say, "Whatever happened to chivalry? I would do this for you whether you could walk or not!"

The Digmanns have been incredibly fortunate with an immense support system. They are blessed with many friends who have been there from the beginning, as well as the new army of like-minded activists that they have amassed through their many ways of reaching out to others.

Dan: We don't stop. We have a good core group of friends. The accommodations that they make for us are great. People have even built ramps just so Jennifer can get in their house. It's amazing how gracious friends have been to find ways to include us. We also often host gatherings here because it's accessible. We like that this is where everyone chooses to hang out.

Jennifer: I have connected with a lot of people on the internet. There are many people who we've never met face to face, but who we consider our friends. I have a better social life now than when I was in college! I have people who have stuck by me for twenty years with the MS Walk. Even if you can't leave the house there is a community where you can fit in online.

The couple also developed a blog to connect with others in the MS Community.

Dan: A friend of ours encouraged us to do our blog. The writing turned out to be a good escape for me. We started to do some public speaking and what writer doesn't have a dream of writing a book? There was a professor at CMU who wanted to include us in the book she was writing. Ten minutes into the conversation she said we needed to write our own and so we did!

This suggestion lead to the couple's wonderful book, *"Despite MS to Spite MS"*. The collection of essays on living with Multiple Sclerosis is available on Amazon and has provided others with insight, inspiration and most of all, hope.

Dan: We wanted to give people hope but at the same time we didn't want to sugarcoat anything. We wanted to share ways that we have moved ahead in spite of the disease in hopes that it will inspire or help someone else to do the same.

Jennifer: When I was diagnosed there wasn't a lot of positive information or stories about MS. There were certainly none about a woman in a wheelchair. We just felt like we needed to share our stories of hope.

Writing the book together has helped them grow as a couple and to learn more about one another as individuals.

Jennifer: I can't believe how incredibly patient and kind he is. It shouldn't surprise me because those were two of the things I was really attracted to in the beginning, but this disease has been a monster. Even when I am at my worst he is patient with me.

Dan: I can't believe she's put up with me for nine years! And how strong she is to deal with all the stuff that she deals with. It surprises me that she is so understanding of me and how she takes the time to see things from my perspective. She's honest enough to say sometimes that my positive attitude annoys her but she still listens to me.

Jennifer: One thing I disliked about him was that he was crazy about Bruce Springsteen. Nine years later I've seen eight concerts and I'm a big fan, too!

Keeping things in perspective is imperative when you are dealing with serious illness. Sometimes you have to make sacrifices. There are days when you don't have the energy or ability to accomplish everything that you would like to but beating yourself up about it isn't going to help the situation. Having someone beside you who understands that fact makes the unfolded laundry or the dusty end tables seem much less important.

Jennifer: I think MS has helped us to not sweat the small stuff. So what if the dishes didn't get done last night? We were able to spend time together. So your dry cleaning didn't get picked up today but you're able to walk an extra mile. In the grand scheme of things the little annoyances mean nothing.

When you let go of the petty irritations in life you begin to appreciate the joy of life. Dan and Jennifer find something to look forward to every single day and they treasure each experience as if it were priceless.

Jennifer: I am looking forward to Dan finishing graduate school in May. I look forward to him being able to sit on the couch and watch TV with me again. I look forward to waking up with him every day. I know it sounds cheesy but it is absolutely true.

Dan: I can't wait until I graduate either. It will be with a degree in humanities. Jennifer and I started the program together. We took the first couple of classes together but I couldn't fit it in my schedule at the time. I had to bow out. She went on and got her degree in May of 2013 and we went out to the bar with some friends to celebrate. She was talking with one of my co-workers and she looked at me and said "Now it's your turn." I refocused and busted my hump to get that done!

A spouse that encourages you to strive to be your very best self is a gift. He or she allows you to grow. Dan and

Jennifer have the ability to push each other to reach goals and support one another along the way; an ability that will allow them to achieve whatever dreams they have.

Dan: Truth be known, I was always jealous of Jennifer. She had a focus in her degree that kind of drove and influenced what classes she would take. She focused on disability theory, which was awesome. For me, I figured out I was really more inspired by the power of music to influence people's emotions. All of the research I'm doing is surrounding Bruce Springsteen. That's kind of the driving factor behind the classes that I take. When I was diagnosed, I had developed a friendship with one of the sisters of St Clair. I wrote a twenty page letter to her explaining how Springsteen's music helped me come to terms with my diagnosis of MS. I would love to meet him someday.

Jennifer: I don't think Dan could ever meet him. His head would explode!

The wealth of wisdom that this couple has gained throughout their journey is a gift that everyone diagnosed with a chronic illness should be as lucky as to receive.

Dan: Have faith in yourself and your relationship. You can make it through this. Just go forward understanding that it's not always going to be easy. Jennifer has had MS for seventeen years and there are still new challenges to face. You need to give yourself some latitude to come to terms with all of it and make adjustments. But you can make it through it together. You need each other.

Jennifer: There is a mourning process you go through after being diagnosed. I don't want to say a part of you dies but you are not just going to get this diagnosis, cry a couple days, and get better.

But having her "treasure" beside her to dry the tears has made the pain and disappointment of Multiple Sclerosis bearable.

Jennifer: You go through the whole process together and you need to develop a "we can handle this" sort of attitude. It has to be you two together taking on the world. Dan is my partner in crime. I have to lean on him. We were just saying they should call it "Multiple Sclero-us".

Mark & Lynn Forrette

M̲ark and Lynn Forrette discovered on a river rafting trip that they were a great team when it came to navigating their way through rough waters. Little did they know what a metaphor that trip would be for the challenges they would face together in the future.

It was 1987 and the two were among an assorted group of friends looking forward to an adventurous weekend in Yosemite. They had never met before and Lynn, a divorced woman with two teenagers was immediately attracted to the tall, handsome bachelor with the warm smile. Mark, an athletic outdoorsman was also a bit smitten when he was introduced to the vivacious and energetic Lynn. The two ended up dancing and laughing the night away.

They soon learned they had many things in common including the fact that they were both were nurses and possessed a passion for the field of medicine. But when Mark found out that Lynn was just as crazy about skiing as he was, he decided that a day on the slopes would be a perfect first official date.

Mark: I said I would pick her up at 5am. That next morning however it was pouring rain and windy as heck. I was thinking that there was no way we were going to go. But when I arrived at her house she was standing on the front porch with all her gear, ready to hit the slopes. I was really impressed with her enthusiasm.

The two began spending more time together enjoying many adventures. On a cruise for Lynn's mother's 80th birthday Mark asked for Lynn's hand in marriage. With rings and fancy duds in their suitcases they thought they could easily pull off the ceremony right away with the help of the ship's captain. However they were disappointed when they learned that he was not licensed to perform marriages. Fortunately they found an accommodating retired priest on the ship who was willing to conduct a non-denominational service for a Jewish bride and a Catholic groom.

Lynn: I had brought along a dress that I had picked out awhile back for the cruise. Unfortunately I didn't realize I had gained a little weight. When I put it on I felt like a pink stuffed sausage. Thankfully my mom had fallen asleep in her chair and wasn't offering any criticism.

But it wasn't just her ill-fitting dress that posed a problem. The couple had failed to secure a marriage license beforehand. While they were now married in the eyes of God, in front of an aging theologian and a snoozing mother, the whole affair was not recognized by the state of California. It would be twenty long years before they actually handled that small detail.

The marriage, like the courtship, was filled with sports, vacations and musical concerts.

Mark: There were a lot of interests we shared that kept us on the go. We liked to kayak and bike and hike. That cohesiveness worked really well for us.

It was on a medical trip to Haiti in 2006 that Mark began to worry about a nagging problem he had noticed.

Mark: We were on this really narrow slippery path, backpacking up to this remote site and I kept tripping. There was definitely something weird about my right foot. It wasn't the first time either. Previously we were skiing down a hill that I had done dozens of times. I fell hard when I went to turn and my right leg didn't do what it was supposed to do. It scared me a lot.

Mark had had a long-standing back problem and was scheduled to have back surgery. His surgeon, however, wasn't certain that all of the issues were a result of his spinal damage. After the surgery his symptoms did not improve. That's when Mark, armed with a nurse's curiosity, began to research other possibilities. It wasn't long before he literally diagnosed himself with Multiple Sclerosis. Initially Mark's neurologist didn't concur however. Over the course of several years, Mark endured numerous MRI's, as well as other diagnostic work. Eventually they did find the lesions that would prove that Mark's theory was correct.

I think about today. Mark is doing great right now. If that changes tomorrow, we'll deal with it tomorrow.

Mark: I have an inquisitive mind when it comes to medical issues. When something doesn't make sense to me I want to figure out why. It's not so cut and dry as you've got these symptoms, so you've got this disease.

162

When the tests confirmed a diagnosis of MS, Lynn and Mark were to also learn that Mark had the most aggressive form of the disease, Primary Progressive Multiple Sclerosis.

Lynn: I am really an upbeat and optimistic person. Right now only his legs are affected. There's no point in worrying about what could happen next.

Mark: I think the biggest overall fear I have is of the future. Because my disease is progressing and there is no set agenda for when something is going to occur. When will I stop being able to walk? When will I start to have problems with my bowel and bladder? When will I start to decline cognitively? There is no set time table so it's the fear of the future that really gets to me.

During his long career in nursing Mark had had many interactions with people facing serious illness. One woman in particular left a lasting impression that would have a significant impact on those early days after his diagnosis. She had been diagnosed with Primary Progressive MS as well. Her life and career had been very fulfilling. She had a PhD, she was teacher and she loved to garden. Faced with a disease that threatened to take all of that away she attempted suicide.

Mark: Right after the diagnosis I was fairly depressed but I think I've gotten out of that and I'm handling things pretty well now. I still have frustrations. But those frustrations were a big part of my depression when I was diagnosed. I didn't think I was going to be able to handle it. I certainly understand how someone who had this happen could think about ending their life. At first I didn't want to live this way. A huge part of being able to get past that is Lynn. No pity party here today.

Lynn: You're just in a wheelchair. It's fine. Get on with your life. Sure, I feel bad that he got MS. He is such an outdoorsy guy. It's not fair, but then life isn't fair.

And get on with it they did. The couple bought a specialized van for Mark to drive, remodeled their home to make it accessible and Mark began to explore new hobbies. To Lynn's delight, he became passionate about cooking.

Mark: When we first got together I found out that Lynn is a really fabulous cook. When MS caused me to begin spending more time in the house I started to think that I should spend more time in the kitchen. I had an interest in the culinary arts in the past. As a bachelor I had to cook a lot but then I stopped when we got married. All of a sudden I found this passion within myself for cooking again and it felt good. I will tell you that there are days when I am really pissed off about this disease and I hate MS for what it's taken from me. I have always had this image of myself as someone who would be skiing and hiking into my 70's. But I have been able to develop my cooking. I really enjoy photography and I am exploring that too. These have been very positive experiences. The truth is that they are a direct result of me getting Multiple

Sclerosis. Maybe I can't get out there and bike or do some of the things I used to do, but this is a new chapter in the book.

Lynn: Boy is it ever a new chapter! Last night we had lamb meatballs with caramelized onions and squash with tomatoes. And before that he made homemade ravioli stuffed with asparagus and ricotta and parmesan. He even made lemon curd last week so we had lemon soufflé for dessert! We've known each other for a long time. I can look at him and know what he's thinking. But I am surprised about him developing these new interests. He has stuck with the cooking, and went to photography classes, and had two articles in the paper last week. I give him a lot of credit for going forward. All these new skills that he's gained are amazing. He would not be doing any of these things if he hadn't contracted MS. I say to him over and over "I would rather have you the way you are than any other man I have ever met."

While turning over the kitchen duties wasn't difficult at all for Lynn she admits that she hasn't always been able to stand back and allow Mark to adjust to new ways of completing tasks. Many couples living with MS grapple with the challenge of being helpful as opposed to be overly concerned about how efficiently things get done.

Lynn: Mark always says that when he needs help he'll ask for it. I want to help him because it's way faster. I know that it is for selfish reasons that I want to do things for him. I am the most impatient person in the world. MS is teaching me patience though.

I have to stand back and wait. I am constantly monitoring my speed.

Lynn is not the only one who is developing new coping skills. Going from being a get-it-done kind of man to someone who is willing to accept that he is no longer able to be as autonomous as he once was has been a difficult transition at times for Mark.

Mark: I think that for anybody who has a disability it's a learning process. I am trying to determine what my boundaries are. I feel like if you start something you have to finish it. I'm just not comfortable asking somebody to help me. I'm working on that, but it's all a work in progress. I was so fiercely independent. Over time I am getting better and Lynn has been so good about helping me with that. Thankfully we are able to talk about those issues. Some of it has been kind of tough, like when she helps me even when I don't think I need to be helped or when she has to open the door for me. But being able to talk about it helps.

"When one door closes another opens" is a phrase that seems to apply quite often to the strong marriages that MS sometimes produces.

Lynn: I think we are both a little more patient that we used to be. We are much closer and feel way more connected than before MS entered our lives. There is nothing I can't talk to him about and hopefully he feels the same way. He knows when I am angry or sad or happy or glad. He'll be in a mood and we'll talk about it. We

166

bicker. We like to bicker and that's not bad. We really love each other a lot but we are both always right. There has never been a more stubborn man on the planet.

Mark and Lynn are both very social people and love getting together with friends. As Mark's MS has progressed getting out has become more problematic at times though.

Mark: We have a group of friends who are just so supportive of us. A good example is a couple who lives close by. I didn't think I could get my wheelchair over the threshold of their house so they had a carpenter come and build a ramp! I have received amazing support. I wasn't sure how friends would react, but honestly, they have been really great.

But both of them realize that Lynn needs to carve out some time for herself, to occasionally leave behind the challenges of caring for an ill spouse.

Lynn: Many times he's too tired to go out in the evening or there are too many stairs. And then I am torn. I feel guilty going without him. If it's something I really want to do, I still go. If it's something that doesn't really matter, I stay home. I am going to Nepal in November and I am leaving Mark alone. I want to find more places that are accessible for him. Recently we went to Disneyland and were pleasantly surprised to discover that the entire place is accessible!

Their willingness to adapt to their changing circumstances make Mark and Lynn worthy adversaries of Multiple Sclerosis. However both of them are painfully aware of the ultimate price the disease may extract.

Lynn: Neither one of us want to be on this planet if we can't have something like a full life. We're not religious. We have no grandiose ideas about the after-life. Mark is still able to do all the things he loves, like cook and listen to music. If he gets to the point where he decides he's done however, I will support that. It's about your choices in life. It has nothing to do with MS.

Mark: I think you need to be able to be real about yourself. You need to understand who you are as a person, how you exist on the plant and how you exist in relationships with other people. If you can find a comfort zone there you will be better able to deal with this disease. I tell people that in the poker game of life I got dealt a pretty shitty hand and don't have many chips left. But I'm still in the game.

While unlucky in the game of life, with each other, Mark and Lynn have found a winning hand. Their love has been in no way diminished by Multiple Sclerosis. Even the physical aspect of their life together has remained robust. They both cherish the intimacy they share and have worked to keep it a vital part of their relationship.

Lynn: You have to be kind and understanding. You will have plenty of time to express your own fears, but this is a huge life change for the person you love and they are dealing with it at a much deeper level than you are, so just be kind. We're all shells. It's what's in our heart that's important - not the way our body works.

Ann & Michael Bunting
Rebecca & Marty Kuchar

❧

When you picture two parents standing over their newborn you imagine them cooing over her father's eyes and her mother's perfect button nose. New parents are often thrilled when they discover that their baby has inherited their best traits. On the other hand, some parents worry that they might have passed on a tragic legacy. That fear was very real for Ann and Michael Bunting.

In the fall of 1966, however, children and genetic traits were far from either of their minds. They were both college students at Eastern Michigan University. Ann lived in the same dorm as Michael's sister, Colleen.

Ann: Michael's sister introduced me to him. He has huge blue eyes and I was immediately attracted. His sister was such a lovely person, so I thought he must be wonderful as well. And I was right. From the very beginning he treated me like a queen.

Michael: She was one of the good looking ones. In a campus full of women, she stood out. We double dated the first time and it just went from there. I really lucked out.

It wasn't a whirlwind romance. The couple took their time and explored their options before deciding that they couldn't live without each other.

Ann: We dated for four and a half years and in between time, we dated other people. But we always came back to one another.

You can learn a lot about someone in four and a half years. Michael and Ann discovered early that they were able to weather difficult situations and come out stronger than before.

Mike: I worked my way through school as a sheriff's deputy. Ann was one of the only gals who would put up with me. We had our ups and downs and rounds and rounds like everybody does. I was in the ROTC and due to be shipped to Vietnam. Ann and I became engaged a couple months prior to my deployment. I put her ring in a rose and gave it to her and away we went. I left for the army just after we got engaged back in March of 1971.

With Mike on active duty there wasn't time to plan a big wedding. They were married in June in what Ann calls "one of those shotgun weddings." The ceremony did however include a song that, unbeknownst to them at the time, would become the theme to their life. On the lawn of the college campus Ann walked down the aisle to the haunting melody of *Bridge over Troubled Waters*.

Two years later the couple began to notice the first ripples in those waters.

Mike: I came back from the army and the first problem I noticed was tremors in my right hand. It was significant because I was a platoon leader and I had to make a lot of salutes with my hand. I just couldn't control the tremors. They made it very difficult to do properly. I dropped a gallon of paint on the carpet in our house too. I simply lost control of it. I had difficulty with fatigue and muscle control as well. I used to run a mile around the school but one day I was running my mile and I just collapsed. I couldn't figure out what was going on.

Although the symptoms he was experiencing were troubling to both Mike and Ann, they were very sporadic. At one point along the way a doctor had mentioned the possibility of MS but it wasn't until a neurologist did a spinal tap twelve years from the onset of those disturbing symptoms that he was officially diagnosed with Relapse Remitting Multiple Sclerosis.

We both wondered what the limitations would be so we just banded together and took on whatever the future held.

Ann: We had never heard of MS before so I didn't really know the ramifications. My sister is a nurse and she has helped me out a lot. Our youngest daughter, Kathleen was two at the time and our older daughter, Rebecca was seven. We decided not to have any more children because we didn't know what the future was going to bring. I was only a part-time teacher. I didn't know what we were going to do.

The worry of an uncertain future wasn't Ann's alone. Michael also wondered how this was going to change all of their lives and the expectations that they had for themselves as well as each other.

Mike: I was concerned about the ramifications of the disease and what the future would hold. I had a hard time cutting the grass and doing normal things around the house because of the tremor in my hand. The whole future outlook was cloudy.

But Ann never questioned that she would stand by her husband to face the unknown.

Ann: We have always been very supportive of each other. I told him not to worry. I would never leave him. I love him to the ends of the earth. Although we were sure about our love, we didn't know how others would react to his illness.

After initially encountering some disheartening reactions and comments from people close to them, the couple decided to keep Mike's illness a secret as long as they could. They also chose not to tell their young daughters.

Rebecca: I always thought my Dad had a bad back. I remember when I was in 2nd grade he couldn't go to the daddy-daughter date night which still makes me sad. I didn't understand why he slept so much and why he didn't feel well.

Although Ann doesn't remember telling Rebecca about the real reason behind her father's ailments, Rebecca recalls the moment with perfect clarity.

Rebecca: I can remember that conversation like it was yesterday. My dad was listening but he didn't think I could see him. My first reaction was wondering if he was going to die. I was terrified that he would die. That was before the internet so it was hard to get any information about the disease. I also grew up in the era when

AIDS was first discovered. Some kids wouldn't play with me because they thought they would catch MS.

Even as Mike's health declined the couple assumed his job was still stable. Unfortunately it became a battle to keep it. He was still enlisted in the army part-time as what he called a "weekend warrior" and he was also building a business as an insurance agent. Although Mike's clients had no idea that he was stricken with MS, his superiors got wind of it. At a time when his livelihood was of the utmost importance they fired him.

Mike: First of all they didn't even know what Multiple Sclerosis was or what the impact would be. Secondly, with all due respect to them, they were jerks. They gave me a hard time. The clients didn't but they sure did. I got a hold of an attorney and he thought I had a legitimate case. My employer ended up letting me continue but I could only service my existing clients. That forced me to start a second business.

Although Mike's symptoms made it increasingly difficult for him to attend to his two business ventures he did everything he could to remain in the workforce.

Mike: Over the years I started having problems with my legs and then the fatigue became significant. I also had problems with vision and driving at night. We just hung in there and took every day as it came. My clients stayed with me, most of them for twenty years, which I can't thank them enough for.

His employers weren't the only people who disappointed the couple with unkind reactions to Mike's illness. Sometimes perfect strangers made comments that caught them both off guard. Ann was often the recipient of people's cruel remarks and perceptions.

Ann: It's been very hard on me watching someone who I love be treated so badly by others. When we're out in public I can see people staring at us. One time a woman actually said to me, "I'm surprised you take him out."

It is a sad commentary on today's society that strangers are more likely to approach an animal in a friendly manner than they are a disabled person.

Ann: We currently have a service dog so now I go in to places and Mike stays outside. People stop and talk to him because of their interest in the service dog. But without the dog he's often ignored.

But unfortunately strangers weren't the only people in their lives who ignored Michael.

Ann: As far as friends, many of them have dropped us. You usually do things as a couple. They didn't invite us places because it's kind of cumbersome with Mike in a wheelchair.

Thankfully Ann's family banded together to make things easier for the couple whenever they could.

Ann: I grew up in a family of six kids with an Irish mother. We always stuck by each other and when somebody was sick we took care of them. I don't know what I would do without my brothers and sisters. My brothers take care of the manly things that I can't do. But Michael's family (sigh)...they see him in a wheelchair but I just don't think they know what to do.

Maybe it was growing up in that type of family that prepared Ann for the role as Mike's caregiver. She manages to successfully straddle the thin line between helping and fussing over him, allowing Mike to get what he needs without making him feel as though she is coddling him. It is a skill she has honed over the years.

Ann: I don't think I overprotect him, but I do take care of him as far as adapting the house as best we can.

Mike: She doesn't make me feel like a burden at all.

While Ann had little trouble adjusting to the role of caregiver for her husband, for Rebecca it was an ongoing mourning process as she watched her father lose more of his ability to actively participate in her life. Her sister was six years her junior and had always known her dad to be limited in his mobility.

Rebecca: It was different for me because I remember him walking and healthy and vibrant and strong. Our father's illness was always a part of Kathleen's relationship with him. In my experience Multiple Sclerosis was a disease that took him away from me. But for her, he had always been a man with a disability. The two of us suffered the loss in very dissimilar ways.

As she matured Rebecca was able to absorb the lessons she learned growing up as a child of a parent with Multiple Sclerosis. Her mother and father provided her with a beautiful model of what real love looks like. The experience gave her the tools she would someday need to build one of her own.

Ann: A lot of marriages fail even when illness is not a factor. But our union is very strong and I think it's because of the challenges we faced together. People say illness will either drive you apart or bring you closer. We have become closer than most couples. He's my best friend as well as my partner in marriage. You have to like someone as well as love them. I would never trust anyone like I trust Mike.

Mike: First of all, do what you said you would do. You take the good with the bad, the rich with the poor, healthy or unhealthy. Do what you've got to do to get through. Use whatever resources are available. Fight the good fight. It may sound simplistic, but just like she says, she's my best friend. She decided to stay with me which is unbelievable. We've been together for forty-three years so we've seen the high side and the low side. We're just truckin' on. We decided that we are gonna face together whatever the future brings.

But little did they know how severely that optimism would be tested in the ensuing years. The cruelest blow would not be delivered in the form of additional health challenges for Mike.

It was to strike their precious daughter.

But the tragedy was still years away when Rebecca was in her early twenties and took the optimistic step of joining an online dating service. It was through that means that she was introduced to Marty Kuchar.

Marty: One of the luxuries of online dating is that you get to know someone a little more before your first date. We learned that we had some mutual friends and they vouched for both of us. Our first date was somewhat of an unconventional one. We went to a Lions football game that started early in the morning and then we went out to dinner. It was a very long date but it was the best first date I ever had.

Rebecca: I just remember thinking that our conversation was going so easily. We ended up running into a lot of friends at the game. We really clicked. I think what sealed it, though, was that as we were on our way to the game I spilled a cup of coffee on myself. He asked if I wanted to turn around and change and I said no. He got the biggest kick out of the fact that I was willing to walk around with a coffee stain on my shirt in order to get to the game on time.

Four weeks later the couple was enjoying an evening together at Marty's house, listening to records and playing pool.

Rebecca: He was at the pool table and I was changing records. I had just put on a Bob Seger album when it hit me that I loved Marty. I don't fall in love easily but it hit me like a ton of bricks.

I knew right then that I would spend the rest of my life with him. We were engaged six months later.

Marty: I had a wedding ring in my pocket for a couple weeks straight. Literally every place we went I had it just in case some spontaneous moment came up. It wasn't as romantic as Paris, we were just in my house having a conversation about where our life would go, when I decided it was as good a time as ever and I finally proposed.

While Marty had no doubts about his love for this dark-haired beauty, he was concerned about some odd physical symptoms that were plaguing her.

Rebecca: At twenty-six I started experiencing these horrible episodes of vertigo where I would pass out and when I woke up the whole room would be spinning. I couldn't walk or move. My doctor ordered a CT scan, and because of my father's diagnosis, I asked the tech if he saw any sign of Multiple Sclerosis. I have to admit that I had always harbored a fear of the disease. I learned later than an MRI was the only test that would have shown it.

Rebecca was also suffering from frequent bouts of overwhelming of fatigue.

Rebecca: Marty called me his little parakeet. He joked that if he put a blanket over me I would fall asleep!

Gradually other symptoms began to appear. Rebecca's legs started to go tingly and numb. At the time the couple was expecting their first child.

Rebecca: I had a bad episode just two weeks after I gave birth to our daughter. That caused me to make an appointment for an MRI.

In Rebecca's mind the procedure was no more than a formality. It was time to finally put to rest her fears about Multiple Sclerosis, to prove that the problems that she was having were due to something far less dire.

Rebecca: I went to have an MRI to prove that I didn't have MS. Afterwards I got coffee and donuts and drove home. I was taking pictures of my one month old baby when the phone rang. It was my neurologist. My heart just sank. I worked in the medical field and knew that if a physician calls you a couple hours after your appointment it is not to deliver good news. I remember his exact words. He said, "Rebecca unfortunately the results of your MRI were abnormal. You have MS. Get your shoes on, you need to go to the hospital. Do you want Detroit or West Bloomfield?"

It was February 4, 2013. Rebecca Kuchar was thirty-four years old. Exactly the same age as her father when he was diagnosed.

Rebecca: I just lost my mind. Thank goodness Marty was home with me because he could stay there with our daughter as I rushed to the hospital. I called my mom first and then I called my sister. By the time I got to the hospital they had both arrived and for four days they never left my side. I had grown up witnessing the dreadfulness of Multiple Sclerosis. It was my absolute worst nightmare come true.

Marty: I didn't quite comprehend what she said. I didn't think they could legally even tell you that over the phone. I was hoping there was room for error. Before she ran out of the house she handed me the phone and told me to talk to the doctor. Because of all the chaos going on I accidently hung up on him. She was throwing clothes into a duffle bag and bawling her eyes out. Then she just left. I knew I couldn't follow her because we had an infant that needed me too. I also knew that this was the worst day of her life. It was agonizing not to be by her side.

But Marty was not the only one in agony. Along with attempting to contain her growing panic over the diagnosis that she had just received, Rebecca was struggling with the anguish of knowing that the moment would come when she had to tell her father that she now had the same disease that had taken so much from him.

Rebecca: I was so scared to see my dad because I didn't want him to think this was his fault. I didn't know what to say to him.

Rebecca's mother was suffering her own kind of nightmare. Now not only her husband but her beloved firstborn daughter had become another victim of this monster called Multiple Sclerosis. The stress of the heartbreak was overwhelming, causing even the hair of her eyebrows to fall out.

Ann: I'm still not handling it very well. Every time I think about it I start to cry again. She's my baby. She has be okay.

Mike: I was brokenhearted when we found out that Rebecca had been diagnosed with Multiple Sclerosis as well. However when I was first diagnosed there were no treatments. They couldn't do anything to help me. Since then many more treatments have become available. Becky will hopefully not suffer any of the problems that I have as far as the walking and fatigue. Now they have so many medicines to treat the effects of this disease. Hopefully her future looks a whole lot brighter than mine.

Rebecca: I think in the back of my mind I have always known I was going to get this. When they told me there was a little voice in my head that said "it's here." I felt like I had been running from MS my whole life and it finally caught up with me. Then I got really angry and I started to fight.

But fighting Multiple Sclerosis was actually something that Rebecca had been doing for much of her life. Now the battle just took on a more personal meaning. Rebecca and her uncle had developed an MS Bike team called, "Team For Mike".

Rebecca: All during my twenties I had been advocating and speaking and fighting for my dad. I knew I would not hide the fact that I now had the disease like my father had been forced to do. There was no way I could continue to fight for my dad and not disclose that I had it too.

Fortunately the news was received in a far different fashion by her supervisor. She faced none of the prejudice that her father had to endure.

Rebecca: My employer was incredibly receptive and helpful. There was never a doubt that it wouldn't be an issue. Even when I started a new job I disclosed my illness during the interview process. I'm not ashamed. It's not my fault and I don't have to hide it. I tell them and explain Multiple Sclerosis before they make their own assumptions. I am still working full time and contributing to my job. I refuse to let Multiple Sclerosis affect my career.

After Rebecca was diagnosed the family changed the name of their team to the "Fighting Shamrocks" in order to represent both father and daughter.

Rebecca: We are very Irish and we are fighters so that why we chose the name. We have raised over 100k for research. We have teams all over the country. We even have a federal trademark. We really see this not just as a fundraising arm, but as an advocacy and support group. I talk to four or five people a month who are newly diagnosed. It really is a movement. We have hundreds of people who are involved. Ultimately I am doing it all for my daughter. I will chew my left leg off before I ever let MS touch her.

Her husband, Marty, is also a vital part of the operation.

Marty: My role is to provide support wherever it is needed. Becky is running the ship. I am one of the deck hands for sure. I handle everything from organizing to bringing a generator so that we can have music at bike rest stops.

Rebecca: You do way more than that! You biked one hundred and fifty miles!

Marty: Oh yeah, I did do that too.

Marty is the type of man who sometimes minimizes his contributions but his support and love for Rebecca is enormous.

Rebecca: I'll be honest, when I first found out I wanted him to leave me because I didn't want him to have to go through what my mom went through. I was terrified of what the future would hold and didn't want to be a burden to him. He looked at me and told me to stop talking. He said that would never happen. He's my rock and best friend. I can't imagine this journey without him. He is my calming spirit and my perfect balance. I'm a little high-strung and always go to the negative. He has kept me above the fold.

> He's my rock and best friend. I can't imagine this journey without him. He is my calming spirit and my perfect balance.

The journey has really shown the young couple how much they could overcome together. Within the span of a year and a half they faced a job loss, the birth of a child and a devastating diagnosis. Such huge life changing events would certainly have derailed a more fragile union.

Rebecca: I think our experience is much different than what my parents had to endure. They did the best they could with what they had. I just can't say how much I appreciate them. It's overwhelming the amount of adversity that was hidden from us. My mom worked three jobs to support us. She's the most unbelievable woman I have ever met. It makes me feel bad because I was such a jerk when I was a teenager.

The determination that was modeled for her has given Rebecca the fortitude to face Multiple Sclerosis like a fierce warrior.

Rebecca: My mom always encouraged me to pull myself up by my own bootstraps. I am a very independent woman because of the example my mother set for me. I will raise my daughter the same way. She will be bold and proud and strong. She will grow up knowing what MS is and she'll be part of our work to find a cure. She'll be at events because I believe in teaching children the power of volunteering and advocacy. And thank goodness, she has such an amazing father who will stand with both of us.

Mike and Ann's example of strength, courage and unwavering love is the road map for Marty and Rebecca's journey. They may choose a few different routes along the way but undoubtedly will end at the same destination.

A life filled with devotion.

Epilogue

Was it serendipity? Fate? Or simply the magic that happens when two fearless and somewhat impulsive women meet. Ronda Giangreco had just finished her speech at a National MS Society awards luncheon in Minneapolis, Minnesota. She was seated at a table signing copies of her book, *The Gathering Table, Defying Multiple Sclerosis With A Year of Pasta, Wine & Friends*, when she was approached by a willowy, young woman with a rather sheepish looking man in tow.

Without much hesitation, Jeanne Lassard announced, "I read your book and my boyfriend says that this is socially incorrect of me to ask, but can I come to your house for dinner?"

The response was immediate. Of course she could. After all, Ronda and her husband Michael had hosted over two hundred people at their home in Sonoma, California during their year of dinner parties. Bringing new friends to their Gathering Table was their idea of a great way to enjoy life. Ronda had been diagnosed with Multiple

Sclerosis in 2008. Michael's mother had died of the disease when he was sixteen. Enjoying life had become a priority for both of them.

Unfortunately, in just a few short weeks, a very serious MS attack would land Jeanne in the hospital for eight long and frightening days. As well, Jeanne's boyfriend, Lance Lindahl, had just accepted a new job. Flying all the way to California from their home in Wisconsin seemed like it was now a dream to be placed back on Jeanne's bucket list.

Fortunately Jeanne recovered and she and Ronda began an online friendship, following each other's escapades and triumphs through their Facebook postings.

Jeanne was busy organizing creative and wildly entertaining means of raising money for the cause, including her extremely popular Karaoke for the Cure Night at a local bar.

Meanwhile Ronda's life was consumed by her speaking engagements and travels. However she had long been concerned with the heartbreaking statistics around the number of marriages that break up after a diagnosis of MS. She and Michael had been presenters at a couple of the National MS Society's *Relationship Matters* retreats and had come away with a determination to somehow do more to help with this serious issue. She thought about writing another book, but hesitated when she considered all the time and effort such a project would require.

Realizing that her new friend had a marvelous gift for writing, Ronda suddenly had an idea. How would Jeanne like to co-author a book with her about couples who weren't simply coping with MS, but had found a way of loving each other even more deeply than before the illness had come into their life?

Jeanne's answer was a resounding, "yes!"

Her tremendously supportive partner, Lance, insisted that this was just the right opportunity for her to make that trip to California after all. She'd just have to make the journey solo.

When she arrived at the Giangreco's home in Sonoma the two talked into the night about their ideas for *A Dose of Devotion, How Couples Living With Multiple Sclerosis Keep Their Love Strong*. It was Jeanne and Ronda's desire that the book would have a positive effect on couples struggling with the challenges of living with Multiple Sclerosis. The sobering truth is that as many as 70% of marriages end after a diagnosis of MS.

They wanted to change that.

Ronda and Jeanne expected to be moved by the poignant stories they would hear. They never imagined that they would be so awestruck by the courage, grace and love they encountered. However during the process of reaching out to couples who were willing to share their stories, they also found couples who had succumbed to the fear, uncertainty and anxiety that comes with the diagnosis.

One man wrote in part, that *"This nasty disease has strained and torn apart our relationship over the years beyond repair. MS has robbed us of our love story."*

That email would come to haunt them both but it also provided the motivation they needed to assure them that the demanding, time-consuming and arduous task they had before them was also the most meaningful one they would ever tackle.

They were right. The long hours of writing, interviewing and editing would ultimately prove to be one of the most rewarding journeys of their life.

We have so many to thank, but none more than the extraordinary men we love. Michael and Lance held us when we sobbed over the stories we heard, ate their dinner alone as we wrote into the night and showered us with support throughout the long months of this project.

We also wish to thank Chandra Grant for her design expertise and generosity. You made us look like pros.

And of course, to each of the couples who shared their story with us - we owe you a tremendous debt of gratitude. We were simply the messengers. You were our muses.

Links

counterpunchwines.com

thefightingshamrocks.com

danandjenniferdigmann.com

incredibleaccessible.com

wheniwalk.com

axsmap.com

thegatheringtable.net

nmss.org